I0483831

Gbox *Presents*

VIDEO
PROFITS

How To Create Massive Profits and a New Stream of Income With Your Video Content

COPYRIGHT NOTICE

All rights reserved. No part of this publication may be reproduced, distributed, or transmitted in any form or by any means, including photocopying, recording, or other electronic or mechanical methods, without the prior written permission of the publisher, except in the case of brief quotations embodied in critical reviews and certain other noncommercial uses permitted by copyright law.

© 2015 by GBOX.

All Rights Reserved Worldwide.

ISBN-13: 978-1511646147

ISBN-10: 1511646144

JOIN US ONLINE

For a bunch of bonus material to help you rocket launch your video empire visit:

www.GboxVideoProfits.com

Gain instant access to epic marketing videos that will teach you:

- More tools and resources for you to improve your video content.

- Bonus pricing strategies with real life case studies to see them in action.

- How this Gbox user makes over $50,000 a month selling online videos.

- How to entice thousands of viewers to view your videos.

We will be releasing more of our best, cutting-edge video selling strategies for boosting your sales and profits. You don't want to miss out! Scan the QR code to join us online.

WANT A FREE GIFT?

We'd like to invite you to take a quick survey so we can learn more about you and your video channel. Go to smarturl.it/1minutesurvey to take the survey and we'll send you a free gift!

Visit smarturl.it/1minutesurvey
For A FREE Gift From box

RAVE REVIEWS

HERE'S WHAT SOME GBOX USERS HAVE TO SAY:

"Gbox has really added a new dimension to my business and allowed me to generate revenue in ways I never thought possible. This book has given me great ideas on pricing, marketing strategies and how to implement Gbox into my business. Thanks to Gbox I have thousands of dollars in my bank I would have otherwise left on the table." — *Scott Morris, Video Marketing Scholars*

"Gbox was exactly what we needed to give our fans what they wanted, plus add to our bottom line. Now we have a thriving online video community that our fans can't get enough of. Thanks Gbox for making this happen – we only wish we'd known about this opportunity years ago!" — *Hull FC, Professional Rugby Team*

"Who would have known that so many people would pay to see my videos, I just didn't know how to reach them. Gbox made it a reality, plus gave me all these awesome marketing tools that I thought I would have had to pay thousands for! It could not be easier." — *Shawn L. Artist/Illustrator*

"Thanks Gbox! This was the perfect boost I needed to make my videos into an actual business. I couldn't believe it was possible, let alone so easy! Your marketing tips and tools sure beat the other video hosting platform I was using before." — *Howard M. Hollywood Film* Producer

TABLE OF CONTENTS

SECTION 4:
The Perfect Pricing Model For Your Videos

FOREWORD

Welcome to your video selling journey!

I come from a corporate background, with more than 25 years of experience holding various C-level roles at significant media companies in the digital media business. Over the years I have seen the world shift and advance in ways I never thought possible.

I have seen many startups fail before they even got off the ground because of their inability to challenge the norm to create something authentic and revolutionary. I have learned that the only way to move forward is to embrace the unknown and help fuel the hearts and minds of the innovators who have the guts to imagine a new world of possibility.

My journey with Gbox began a few months ago as I was looking to invest in promising new companies in the video space. I fondly remember the day that I met with the CEO, Dirk, who was simply buzzing with enthusiasm for the movement he has spearheaded with his company. I knew right away that Gbox was something special.

Dirk and I spoke at length about the unfortunate reality of many creators who are forced to conform to the strict regulations of their hosting platform. As someone who has worked for content companies most of my life, it is clear to me that the restricted number of distribution platforms and monetization options, the inability to reach out directly to their customers, and hefty revenue shares paid to these platforms is often very limiting.

Gbox is a very unique company. The company is unbelievably invested in giving creators power over content distribution, while improving the viewer experience. Gbox represents a bright future for online video. Gbox gives me hope that more and more people will be able to turn their passion into a reality through this empowering model that disrupts the norm.

I imagine a future where anyone and everyone who feels the deeply moving impulse to create has the opportunity to do so. In addition to other solutions and platforms that cater to a purely ad-funded free experience, Gbox opens up the spectrum to much wider monetization opportunities.

The focus of this book is to make the online video space better by supporting creators from the ground-up. You'll see what I mean as you start to get into it. Each section is dedicated to a different aspect of marketing and selling your videos, all centered around helping you to create a thriving community around your innovative content. Everyone on the all star Gbox team, is committed to your success.

I hope you will enjoy the journey.

Thomas Hesse
Digital/Media Executive
and Entrepreneur
Gbox Advisor

INTRODUCTION

We here at Gbox wrote this book to help content creators around the world leverage video selling as a viable revenue stream.

THE FACTS

- Videos increase people's understanding of your product or service by 74% *

- 75% of executives watch work-related videos on business websites at least once a week.*

- Click-through rates increase 2-3 times when marketers include a video in an email.*

- Subscriber to lead conversion rates increase 51% when video is included in the email marketing campaign.*

- More video content is uploaded to the internet in 30 days than all three major U.S. T.V. networks combined have created in 30 years.*

    *FACTS VIA QUICKSPROUT[4], INSIVIA[5], AND DIGITALSHERPA[6].

Clearly video is important and even though your market is potentially huge, your ability to capture that market is determined by knowing how to sell your videos online.
If you want to sell your videos online you need to understand how to bridge the gap between having great content and having people be exposed to it.

THE FORMULA

While many factors determine the success and ultimate revenues of video content, for our purposes it's helpful to start off with a simple model.

Your video's revenue is a function of having a killer video *and* marketing, or:

Revenue = (Killer Video) x (Killer Marketing)

[i.e. your video's revenue is a function of its quality and the effectiveness of your marketing]

So therefore,

Revenue – Costs
Profit = (Killer Video) x (Killer Marketing) – Costs

Ultimately, this book assumes you have the killer video part down - we aim to provide you the insights to maximize your revenue through a killer marketing campaign using the most cost-effective tools available.

For individual creators, Gbox was built on the premise that you should be able to share your video content easily and on your terms. But more than that, if you create awesome content that people love, you deserve to be properly compensated so you can keep creating. No more relying on third party hosting services that take 40% or more of the earnings from your videos. We know how much your videos are worth and we wrote this book to help you make video selling a source of real income.

For enterprise companies, Gbox is a powerful turnkey solution that gives you a new, viable revenue stream through video. Many companies have hours and hours of exclusive footage shot of their sports teams, interviews, events and news broadcasts, and Gbox is your way to monetize this content. With Gbox, you have control over how your content is distributed and you are empowered to build a powerful community behind it.

This book, which is divided into four parts, is your one-stop-shop for starting, developing, and then maximizing your profits through selling online video content.

We take you through everything from identifying your ideal customer to creating a thriving community around your videos. We teach you about marketing funnels, how to reach a larger audience on social media, how to build your email list, and even pricing strategy secrets to maximize your profits.

In the first section on jumpstarting your video business, we teach you about how to sign-up for Gbox, the premier video distribution and monetization platform available today. In minutes you will have your own video channel set up and ready to start making money from your video content.
In the social media marketing section we talk about what sort of content works best on each of the biggest social networking sites. Social media marketing is vast and varied, and we give you our number one tips and strategies focused on how to leverage social media for selling your video content. We also give you the lowdown on how often you should be posting on each network, how to engage each specific audience, and more!

We take our marketing advice one step further by dedicating an entire portion of the book to email marketing. Email marketing is one of the highest converting marketing strategies out there, but it is poorly used by many companies. We teach you the best practices specific to your video business and how to turn your email subscribers into buyers.

Our highest converting tactics stem from building a video sales funnel that prompts opt-ins to your email list, and then leads them to buying. We break down the different aspects of this funnel, and give you the ultimate formula to increase your opt-ins and conversion rates.

The last section of this book talks about pricing strategies. In addition to offering multiple pricing options on the Gbox platform, we have analyzed a number of case studies on our quest to finding the magic formula for pricing your videos. We will teach you how to use this formula to effectively price your videos in a way that maximizes your content's value and your profits.

We are really looking forward to guiding you on your journey to making video selling a viable profit stream for you or your business.

WHO IS THIS BOOK FOR?

This book was created for industries, businesses and individuals who have AMAZING content.

This book was created for anyone from an individual creator to an enterprise entertainment company. The only requirements entail you or your organization having an initial database of people.

We suggest that a healthy database has at least 2,000 to 3,000 people. In addition, you MUST have AMAZING content. This means your audience must love what you do.

If you are someone who has a few videos, or maybe even a video channel, but you don't yet have a devoted following, this book may not be very helpful for you to implement now.

Here are some examples of who we created this book for:

Individual Creators:

These are people who have a passion that they show the world through video. You are an expert in your field and have a large audience of viewers who love your content.

This could be related to makeup, comedy, fashion, DIY, fine arts, fitness and more. You have a passion for video and your following tunes in every time you release a new video.

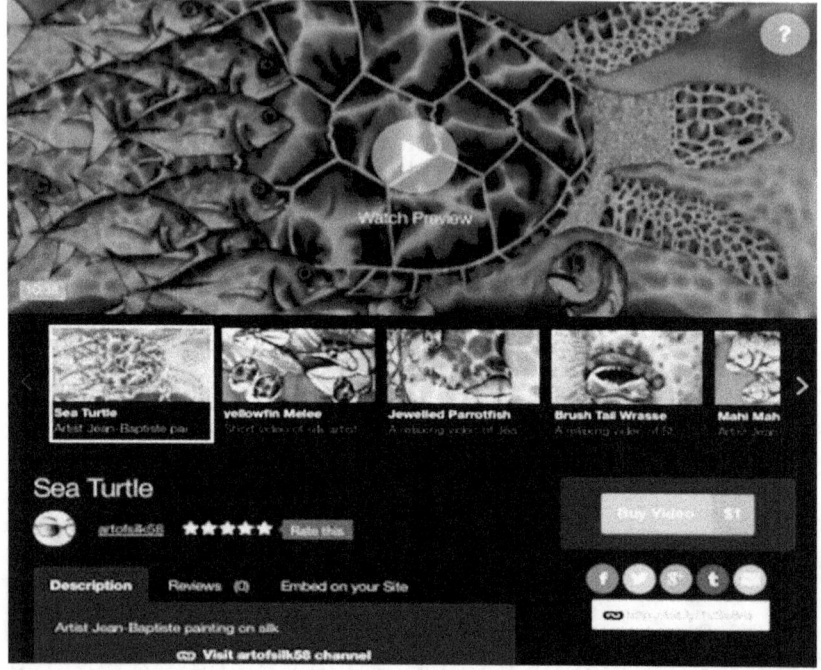

Social Celebrities and Influencers:

These are influencers online who have built a large audience around their niche. You are an industry leader and subject matter expert. You have a passion for educating others in your field and growing your community. A good example of these people includes: Tim Ferris[7], Guy Kawasaki[8], Neil Patel[9], and Sean Ellis[10].

Filmmakers and Film Producers:

You are a filmmaker or producer with amazing content. You have tons of video content and a large following. Gbox provides solutions for VOD channels, syndication partnerships and subscription pricing models (including pay-per-view).

News Media:

You are a publication, a news channel, or a non-profit organization that heavily focuses on news syndication for your audience. These organizations focus on the creation of large amounts of content and turning that content into views. Your audience depends on content from you on a regular basis. You have a large audience and use many fundraising methods to get in touch and involve your audience.

With Gbox you are able to engage your audience using a combination of marketing tactics, email promotions, and our built-in fundraising platform. Fair Observer[11] is a great example of a news company effectively using Gbox to reach a larger audience to sell their online videos.

We will teach you how your audience can be even more involved with your organization through storytelling and other techniques.

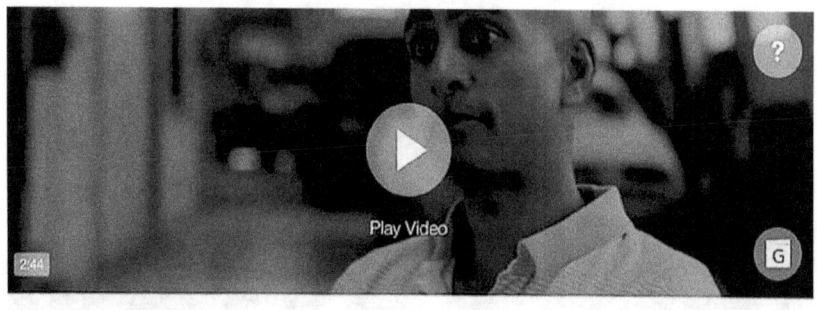

Will millennials read Fair Observer?

Fair Observer   Rate this (2 Votes)

Description   Reviews (0)   Embed on your Site

Atul Singh discusses the ideas and origins of Fair Observer.
http://www.fairobserver.com/

Visit Fair Observer channel

YouTube Users:

Do you effectively use YouTube? Do you have more than 3,000 subscribers? Then you will LOVE Gbox and the flexibility it provides for you. This platform is designed for

people like you who want to make more money from your content and build a direct relationship with your consumers. Gbox helps creators build stronger relationships with their audience. With Gbox you are empowered with that direct consumer relationship.

Sports Entertainment Companies

You are an organization with a huge fan base. The fans want to watch interviews, past and current games/events, athlete profiles and much more. Gbox is a hub for this. Gbox allows you to charge your fan base a certain amount to watch any content you decide to release. This book gives you the ultimate way to engage with your fans.

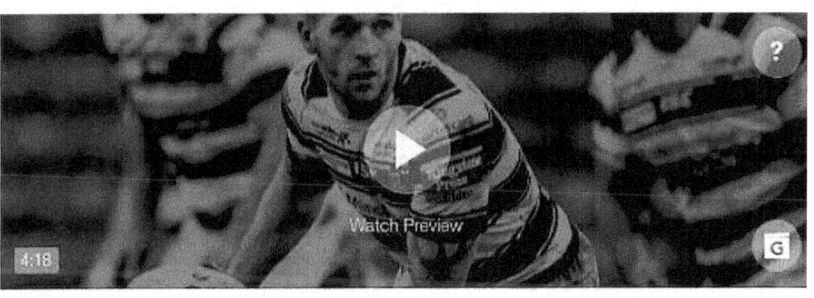

Anyone else!

Anyone who has AWESOME content and a following!

Did we miss you? If you have tons of great content and a large following but were not included in the above list, then you are definitely in the right place. Keep reading!

HOW TO USE THIS BOOK

We start this book by directing you to sign up for Gbox[12] because it is the premier content sharing and monetization platform available today.

We have included screenshots to demonstrate how easy it is to get started on the Gbox platform.

We're going to take you through case studies of actual Gbox creators. We've helped these creators build their video empires using the tools and strategies outlined in this book. We've included screenshots, actual ad and email copy, plus a ton more, in order to illustrate this.

That being said, if you already have your own video distribution channels in place, you will still benefit greatly from this book. The marketing, pricing, community building and brand development strategies we go over are invaluable for all content creators.

We've also included our favorite resources for you to check out in order to make this all happen. The URL for every resource referred to in this book is listed at the end in the "Tools and Resources" chapter. Some of these resources are free to use, and some are paid. We have done our best to make everything in this book work for you, no matter what your budget is.

LET'S GET STARTED!

SECTION 1

Jumpstart Your Video Business With Gbox

Chapter 1: Get Started With Gbox

You have a passion and you have built an incredible video library of content around just how awesome you are.

You have an audience who is interested in the type of information you're providing through the stories, tips, advice and anecdotes in your videos. You make people's lives better with your content!

You are a company with hours and hours of video footage that you distribute through different channels.

However, you don't yet know how to make money from your content.

Fear not! You are in the right place. You have taken a GREAT first step by reading this book.

Now, follow along as we teach you a super simple way to start selling your videos.

We want to show you the best method to sell videos online: using Gbox.

Unlike other services out there, Gbox is committed to the lowest transaction fees because we believe that selling a movie online should not take as much effort as making a movie.

Traditional Distribution:

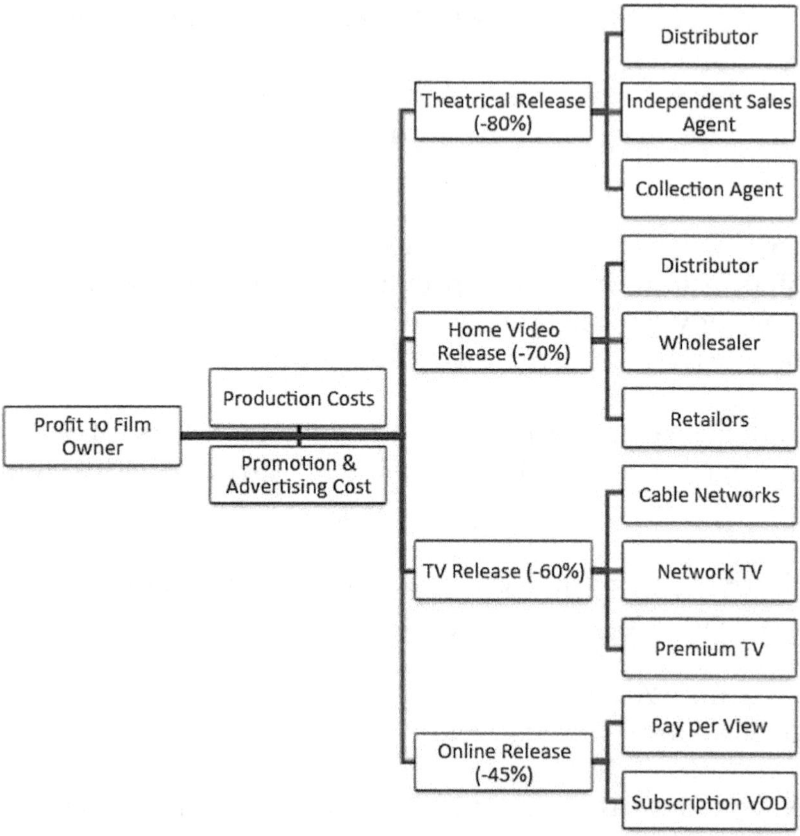

Profit to Film Owner
Production Costs
Promotion & Advertising Cost
Theatrical Release (-80%)
Distributor
Independent Sales Agent
Collection Agent
Home Video Release (-70%)
Distributor
Wholesaler
Retailors
TV Release (-60%)
Cable Networks
Network TV
Premium TV
Online Release (-45%)
Pay per View
Subscription VOD

By setting up an account with Gbox you are developing a direct sales relationship with your viewers.

Gbox Distribution:

Profit to Film Owner
Production Costs
Online Platform
Online Marketing Campaign

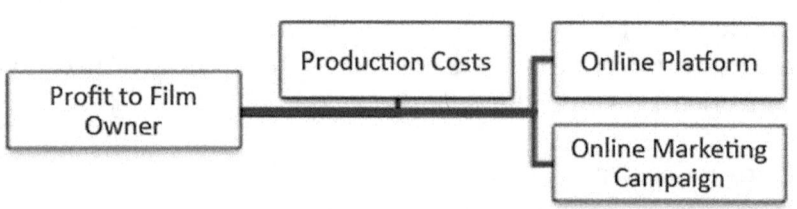

Ready to get started?

Step 1: Sign-Up For A Gbox account.

Yes, it is that simple. Go to **www.Gbox.com** to sign-up for your very own, free Gbox account. Enter your email address and create a password. You can even log-in using your existing social network account on Facebook, Google+, Twitter or LinkedIn.

Gbox is simple to use and puts YOU in control of your video sales. Within minutes you will have an account and a built-in web platform to start making money from your videos. Once you are signed up for an account, move onto the next step.

Step 2: Complete Your Profile

You want to create a profile that presses the "hot buttons" and emotional triggers of your target audience. If you are an organization, click on the "organization" tab next to the "individual" tab.

Some examples of hot buttons: if you are trying to raise money for a non-profit, then you should use a picture that resembles the cause (i.e. children who are hungry; the impact of pollution on the environment, etc.).

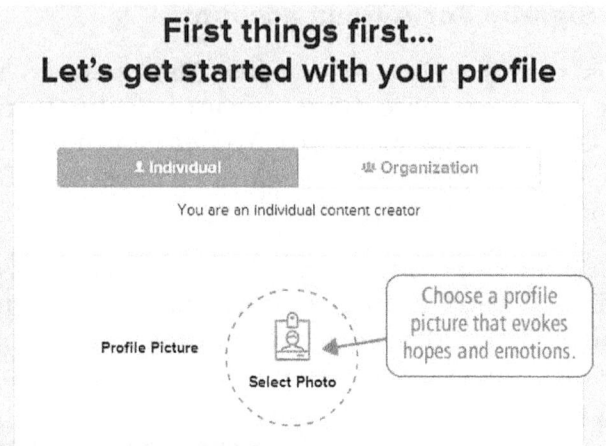

First things first...
Let's get started with your profile

Or, if you are trying to accumulate a devoted audience for your makeup, health or fitness channel, try using a "before/after" picture to show how transformative your skills are. You're a professional in your field? Upload a clear, professional headshot. A well-established brand, entertainer, sports team or news channel? Your logo/branding should go here.

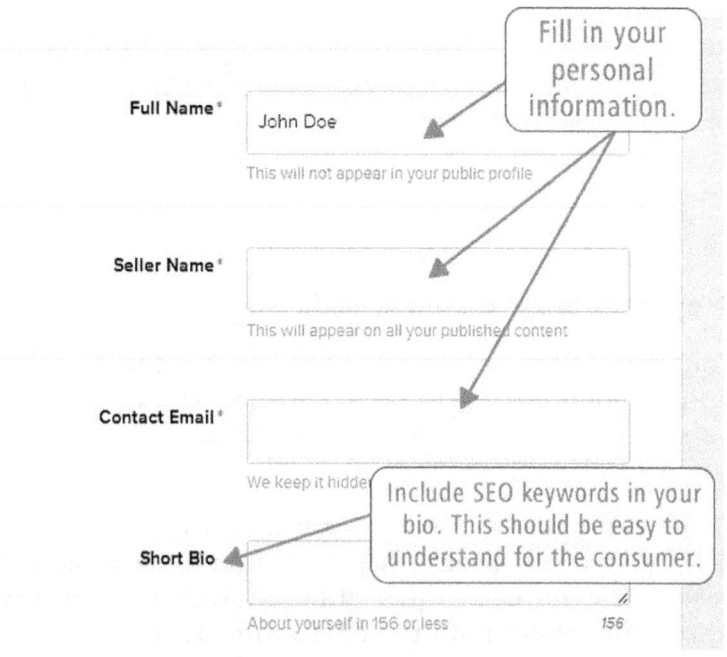

Step 3: Choose A Video

You can upload as many videos as you want to sell - there is no limit! But here is what you want to keep in mind:

- Make sure your video is easy to understand.
- Your video must be high quality with no sound problems.
- Make sure it addresses an immediate problem your consumer is facing.
- If you are making a video just for entertainment purposes, be sure to infuse humor into it.
- Focus on your consumers and what they want. In return they will deliver value.

Chapter 2: Upload & Price Your First Video

Step 4: Upload A video

The next step is to upload your video into the Gbox portal. Doing so allows you to create your own video gallery. Whether you have a website or not, you will still be able to sell videos right from your unique Gbox channel.

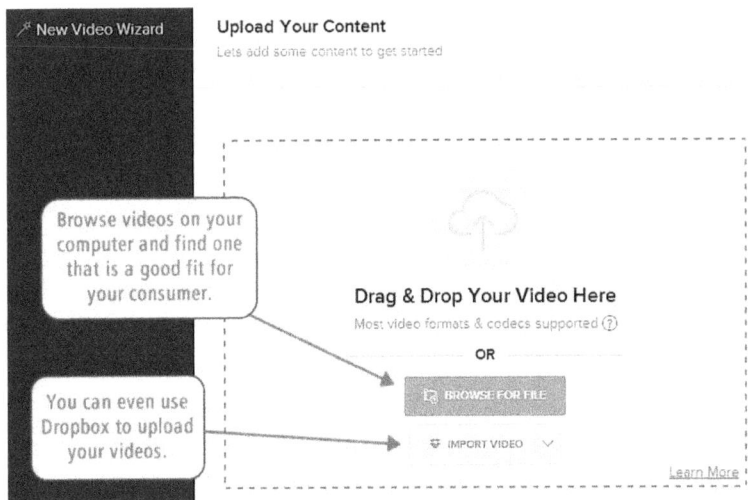

So get going! Start uploading your video content. The more content - the more opportunity for you to make money!

Step 5: Create An Offer

This is where you really have to know your audience. The offer you create is based on their preferences and past purchasing behavior.

If you have never sold one of your videos before, sometimes the best way to find out what your audience is willing to pay for your videos is just by asking them.

Try sending a small group of your most devoted fans a simple email asking them "what is this content worth to you?" Based on their answers, create an offer.

Expert tip: Look up videos from other people who are targeting the same audience as you and see what they are charging for their content.

Start by uploading the video(s) you want to sell.

Then select a cover image that is most relatable to your target audience. This cover image is one of the first things your viewer sees when they come to your page, so you want to use it to convey your core message. If you already have a brand that is memorable, then your logo should be in the image as well.

Create a title using the keywords people will use to find your video on Google. This may require you to do some competitive research. Find out which keywords your competitors are ranking for via SEMRush[13].

The description is the most important part of the process!

Your consumers must know exactly what they are receiving, so make sure it includes popular keywords.

You may want to use UberSuggest[14] if you are having a hard time coming up with 5-6 keywords to use.

Your tags should consist of the 5 keywords that are in your title and description.

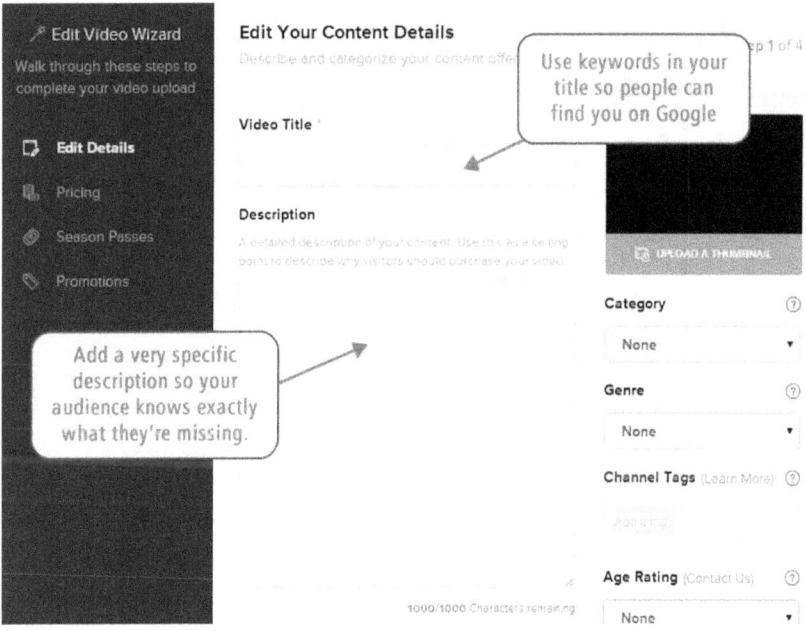

The pricing you want to use is determined by the previous purchasing behavior of your target audience.

• Use the "Fundraising" method when your video is for a cause. For example: If you want help raising money for an event or a philanthropic campaign you're working on. Or, if you're looking for crowdfunding on a new project or initiative, this pricing method is also great to use.

- The "Name Your Price" option should be used when you are unsure of your pricing strategy. This allows the consumers to help point you in the direction of what your content is worth.

- "Fixed Price" should only be used when you are already aware of the purchasing behavior of your target audience.

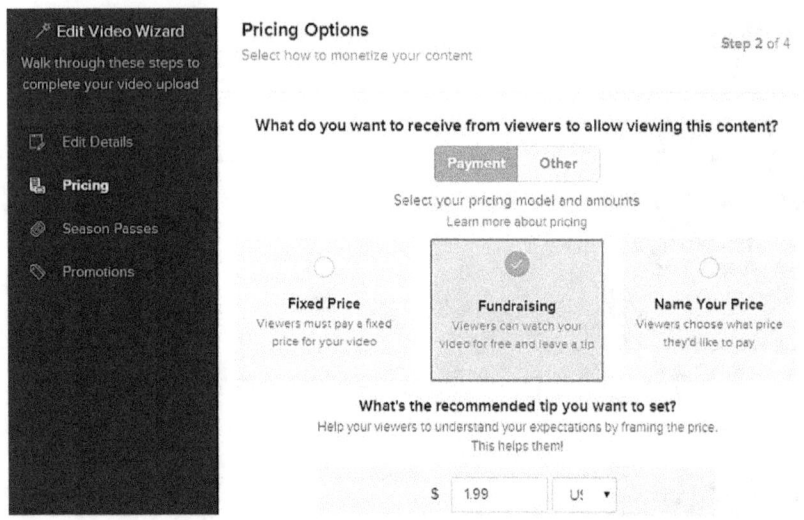

SECTION 4 of this book is dedicated to helping you decide your pricing strategies. We recommend referring to this section if you're having difficulties pricing your videos, or are struggling with your video sales.

Promotional Copies

How many copies do you want to give away for free? You can choose to add promotional copies to each sale of your video. This means when someone pays to watch one of your videos, they can send free copies to their network. If you are confident about your video and the value of it, then you may want to bypass this part. Otherwise choose this based on your promotion initiatives.

Season Passes

Offering different season passes to your viewers is a great way to incentivize your audience to buy. The more time your viewers opt-in for, the cheaper the pass is for them. For example, viewers can opt to view any of your videos for one week for $4.95. Or, they can get a monthly pass for $29.95, or a one-year pass for $49.95! Obviously the most economical deal is the year pass, and all it takes is a click of a button for you to create this deal.

Congratulations! You successfully made it through uploading your first video using Gbox!

Chapter 3: The First Step Of Community Building

Step 6: Email Your List

We are going to be taking you through some seriously in-depth marketing strategies in the next chapters of this book, but to get you started, the first thing you need to do is contact the people already on your list in order to tell them about your video channel.

Here are the 3 stages of a community:

- Friends and Family.

- Friends of Friends of Friends.

- Town Hall – Invite everyone to one place and connect consumers with other consumers.

This is your opportunity to receive feedback on your video from the people who already know you or your brand. Their feedback is a great jumping point from which you can improve future content.

Once they see your video and fall in love with it, ask them to share with their extended networks. This is how you start building a community around your videos.

Community building plays a huge role in video distribution.

When you have created a thriving community around your

video channel, the social proof of your popularity works in your favor to attract even more viewers.

Since it's so important for your video selling success, you'll see the concept of community building referred to throughout this book.

In the next section we will be talking all about social media marketing and how to leverage the various social media sites in order to build a thriving community of engaged viewers. Remember, the happier your customers are with your content, the more readily they'll refer you to their own networks. This is how you increase your profits and create a sustainable revenue stream from your videos.

SECTION 2
Social Media Marketing For Selling Videos Online

Chapter 1: Introduction

Now that you're set up on Gbox and have uploaded some great videos, it's time to add the missing element - the money.

When it comes to converting your viewers into buyers, there are many different tactics and approaches you can take.

One of the biggest converting factors when it comes to video selling is how you leverage social media.

When it comes to your target market, it isn't just about posting updates on all your social network pages and leaving it at that. It is about making that initial connection with your target audience, educating them about how your videos can improve their lives, and then leading them to buying.

Who doesn't want their consumers to keep coming back? That is the goal with social media. This section of the book goes over the step-by-step process on exactly how to create this connection with your target audience.

Since 2006, "Social Media" has been the most talked about buzzword, and using it the right way to achieve your goals is Gbox's initiative. Our success is your success, so implement everything we teach in this book and you are sure to see results with your videos.

The goal with social media marketing is to build a community that people want to be a part of. When your community feels special and cared for, they not only purchase more of your content, but they become advocates for your content, prompting their own networks to join in.

This is the great thing about social media! Your social reach is increased exponentially when you create engaging content that gets people excited.

How To Use This Section

In this section we are going to be taking you through social media marketing tactics you can leverage to increase your conversion rates.

This is an overview of multiple social media strategies, full of tips and tricks we've tested with our Gbox creators, and we're confident you're going to find them very useful.

What You Will Learn

Follow along as we teach you:

- How to effectively leverage social networks to build your online community.
- How to build a social media strategy around selling videos online.
- How to use A/B testing to find out which videos are working and which ones need to go.
- How to attain conversions that turn video selling into a profit stream.
- How to launch an effective social media campaign to help you sell your videos, every time.

What You Need To Know About Selling Videos Online

Video selling and content selling is about exposing your passion. Your passion is what connects you to your audience, and your audience to you.

We want to provide you with the resources you need to connect with your biggest consumers, and then we want to show you how to keep them engaged and coming back for more.

Video selling depends on your consumers. If you give them what they want, they will deliver value in return. The bigger the following you have, the more feasible it will be for you to sell your videos.

The best content builds excitement and awareness amongst your prospects. Then you can use your content to build your video stream around your consumers.

Chapter 2: Create A Strategic Plan

Your strategic plan should be created around the AIDA process:

Attention — the ability to attract the attention of the consumer.

Interest — the ability to raise the interest of the consumer by focusing on benefits and features.

Desire — convinces the consumer that they want to see your video.

Action — consumer is lead towards taking action by purchasing.

The most important part of the process is making your audience aware of your content, which is why social media marketing is so important.

Case Study - Pattie's Pastries

Pattie's Pastries is a great example we can use to give an overview of the entire social media process.

Pattie has a company that sells pastries through an e-commerce website.

Even though she may have the best pastries in town, until she is able to capture the attention of her target market, no one will ever know about them. This is especially tricky since she sells her products online, and her consumers aren't able to do a taste-test before purchasing.

She starts using Gbox to create videos around her "secret recipes" to showcase her skills and get her consumer's mouths watering.

Using Facebook, Twitter and Google+, Pattie shares her Gbox videos to the fans who are engaged on these pages, but haven't necessarily bought her pastries yet.

Pattie's videos appeal to other bakers and pastry chefs, catering companies, plus people who just love pastries!

These consumers vicariously experience her magic recipes through the videos she uploads to her Gbox channel. They watch and share her videos on Facebook, Twitter and Google+.

Pattie is able to catch their interest and direct them to check out her other recipes and inventory on her website. Since her Gbox videos all point to her online store, it's easy for consumers to visit her website and see all of the products she has available.

Now they are ready to click the buy button! At this point she has really piqued their interest and started to build a community around her brand.

Here comes the tough part: you will be evaluated based on what you deliver.

Your biggest prospects and customers will tell the world what you have done for them through a review, comment or even a share on a social network.

These reviews either make or break your business. If you have positive reviews, you start building trust with consumers and attract a larger audience. If you have negative reviews, your consumers will question the quality of your content and this may negatively impact their buying behavior.

Pattie's community writes positive reviews on her videos and social media pages because they are informative and fun to watch.

Consumers who purchase her pastries write and share about their experiences because her pastries really deliver on value. They are delicious, well presented, and delivered to their doorstep in less than 24 hours. All of these factors make for a positive consumer experience, and Pattie's consumers are not shy about sharing their happiness!

Pattie has created a community not only of passive consumers who "Like" her posts and videos - but she has created a community of advocates who share her posts, tell their friends about how delicious her pastries are and recommend her to their networks.

Her audience has grown from her family of five to nearly 18,000 people in the last year alone.

This is the power of content selling!

Jump onboard!

Define Your Objectives

Now let's really dive deep into creating your own social media marketing plan.

Step one is to define your objectives.

What do you expect social media to accomplish for your videos?

Many people have the tendency of jumping into the execution mode without really thinking about their goals.

And even when it comes to their goals, they only think about getting more followers and "Likes." These are called "vanity metrics" and they will not take you anywhere with your business.

The key thing here is your target audience. Yes, it doesn't matter if you have 9 followers or 9,000 followers. The only way to make money from your videos is by selling to your target audience.

What would you rather have? 9 followers who regularly purchase your products, or 9,000 followers who never buy? When people focus on vanity metrics they are easily lead to the belief that social media doesn't work. This is why it is paramount to know what you want to accomplish through social media.

Social media is a great way to accomplish many different objectives. The biggest requirement for achieving your objectives is by putting in consistent effort. Nothing can be achieved with social media overnight.

Think about what sort of objectives you want to accomplish from your social media marketing efforts. For example, some of the most common goals include:

- Lead generation
- Targeted website traffic
- Improving brand reputation
- Building brand awareness
- Selling more videos online!

Increase website traffic: The best way to initiate this is through search engine optimization and getting your videos and posts to show up on the search engine results page. Once you have used social media to develop solid relationships with people who trust you, they will visit your website. Not to mention when you tweet a blog post, video or other link, there is always a chance that it will show up in the search engines. Set a benchmark and monitor it often. Again, this isn't an overnight job.

Reputation Moderation: Social media is the number one place to find out what people are saying about you. You might not believe it, but people rate everything through social media. If they had a completely great experience with you, then they will share it. If it was horrible, people will be sure to share that as well. In the end, social media allows people to learn about things faster than through any other method.

Brand Awareness: Your brand personality will determine who follows you and who doesn't follow you on the web. Your audience is watching your updates. What do you want people to see your company as? They are ready to talk about your brand. The way your audience speaks about your brand will help you determine if your brand awareness is on the right track or not.

Increase Video Sales: Any social media strategy you create should be centered around video sales. This is measured in concrete numbers (views). You can track this through campaign-specific landing pages, coupon codes, and even contests.

Establish Your Key Performance Indicators

How will you know if you have reached your goals through social media or not? This is not an "automated" tactic. Social media requires consistent effort to maintain engagement. You have to stay on top of your audience's activities and adjust to their ever-changing wants and needs. Here are some guiding questions to help you determine your key metrics:

- How many social shares is your content getting? (This is also called earned media when your fans share your content with their friends and connections).

- How many comments is your audience leaving on each post online? How many comments are you receiving on your videos?

- How many ratings do you have on your videos?

- How many friends or followers are you losing on a weekly basis?

- Which keywords are people clicking on the most? Which are not getting many clicks?

- What links are being clicked on? (You can use Snip.ly[15] to check this)

- Are you tracking your linkbacks, pingbacks?

- Is your content leading to sales or increased traffic?

Note how the above list doesn't mention anything about gained followers or "likes." Unless a follower is actively engaging in your content (sharing, commenting, reviewing), just having them as a follower is not helping build your brand or increase your profits.

Your Target Audience

A well-defined target audience will bring you more video sales than you ever imagined. The important step here is to create a profile of your ideal customer. The whole point of this exercise is to identify who your content is speaking to, and then create content your target audience will instantly resonate with.

You want to confront "pain points" to build trust with your target audience.

Think about the tone your audience relates to. Remember, the more you listen to their needs, the better you can respond to their needs. Then you can be positioned as an industry expert in your niche.

While keeping the above considerations in mind, here is the criteria you want to focus on when creating an ideal client persona:

Who is your target consumer?

- Age

- Income level

- Education level

- Relationship status

- Do they have kids?

- Gender

- Ethnicity

Where do they hang out?

- Where are they geographically located?

- What associations are they part of?

- Which websites do they visit?

- Which publications do they read?

- How do they primarily communicate? (Text, Twitter, social media, phone, email, etc.)

What are their likes and what are their dislikes?

- What are their biggest preferences?

- What is their secret desire?

- What are they looking for?

- What is their biggest problem?

- What are they spending their money on?

- What are they complaining about?

After you identify your audience, you want to approach them in an authentic way. If you identify the champion within your consumers and then help them "win" in their lives through your content, they will become ambassadors for life.

Remember, your consumers all have different needs based on their individual context. Once you recognize your prospect's needs, you can create content that is specific to them.

Who Is Your Competition?

Defining your target audience is the first step to success. Now you also need to know your competition. Your competition will give you an idea as to what your competitive advantage is, as well as which tactics your competition is already carrying out.

This will require you to research other organizations and brands in your niche.

Here is what to look for:

- Which networks and sites are they using?

- Who is following them? Or "Liking" them?

- What are people saying about them? (Read their Facebook and YouTube reviews for this).

This is on-going research for your brand, meaning that you shouldn't just do it once and then never again. In order to maintain the competitive advantage when it comes to your competitors, you want to further your research on a weekly basis.

In the next steps, follow along as we show you how to implement the right social media strategy geared to the right prospects. And then learn how to deliver your content at the right time.

Which Social Networks Should I Use?

The social networks you use depend on your audience. For example, Pattie's Pastry business relies heavily on Facebook and doesn't use LinkedIn at all.

She tried using LinkedIn and didn't see much traction, so she concentrates her marketing efforts on Facebook.

Research different groups within the biggest social networks to determine which ones your target audience is using most. Even though you may want to use more than one social network, your target audience is generally using one.

Search for keywords in your industry on different social networks to see what people are talking about in relation to a specific topic in your niche. This will help you determine what you should focus on.

We suggest you pick the top three social networks to be a part of initially, and then once you have been established on those, you can move on to other social networks.

Here is what you want to keep in mind with these networks:

- Be present.

- Be consistent.

- Create content your audience can instantly relate to.

Social Media Site Comparison

Tool	Facebook	Twitter	LinkedIn	Blogs	Flickr	YouTube	Yelp	Foresquare
Text	x	x	x	x			x	x
Photos	x	x	x	x	x		x	x
Videos	x		x	x	x	x	x	
Tagging				x	x	x		
Sharing	x	x	x		x	x		x
Friendship/ Following	x	x	x		x	x	x	x
Rating							x	x
Reviewing							x	x	x
Commenting	x		x	x	x	x	x	x
Checking In	x	x					x	x
How You Can Use It	Custom service, PR,HR/ Recruiting, building personal relationships with customers, encouraging fans to share your stuff, driving site/ blog traffic.	Custom service, PR,HR/ Recruiting, building personal relationships with customers, encouragin g fans to share your stuff, driving site/blog traffic.	Professional networking, PR, HR/ recruiting.	Share your industry expertise, help your site rank better with search engines, control your business's online reputation.	Give your customers another way to find you in search, showing instead of telling – especially good for hospitality, restaurants, retail.	Give your customers another way to find you in search, showing instead of telling – especially good for hospitality, restaurants, retail.	Control your business's online reputation, stay on top of customer sentiment, customer service.	Offer deals for customers near you, give your customers another way to find you (through proximity).
No-No's	Oversharing (keep those party photos off your business page).	One-way conversatio ns that don't listen and respond to others.	Spamming groups with pitches for your business.	Letting them die: keep that content coming.	Failing to tag your photos.	Bad sound quality, lack of valuable content.	Posting positive reviews under a pseudonym .	Checking in everywhere all the time; you don't need to be mayor of a parking lot.
High-Profile Users	Nike, Coke, the New York Times, NPR	Ashton Kutcher, Kanye West, Anderson Cooper, Sarah Palin	Barack Obama, Bill Gates	Seth Godin, Bill Marrlor	The Smithsonian , the British Monarchy, the White House	GEICO, Old Spice, Justin Bieber		Bravo TV, the New YorkTimes
How Big Is It?	~1.19 Billion active users (worldwide)	~232M active users (worldwide)	~332M users (worldwide)	152M worldwide (per Blogpulse)	~87M (worldwide)	~1 Billion active users (worldwide)	15M reviews; 39M monthly visitors in Nov. 2010	~45M users (worldwide)
In One Word	Ubiquitous	Easy	Professional	Storytelling	Pictures	Movies	Opinions	Proximity

The leftmost vertical labels read: "What You Can Do With It" (upper section) and "Things to Know About It" (lower section).

Chapter3: Create A Video Content Strategy Create A Survey

Create A Survey

You have done the research on your target audience. You have done the research on your competition. You have determined what social networks you're going to be using. Now what?

It is time to find out how interested your target audience really is with the content you create. This will determine the purpose of your video content and what your consumers really want from you.

Create a survey to send out to your current list of subscribers to help determine the interest level of your target audience.

Best Practice: In order to increase your survey submissions and get some valuable insight, offer a free gift or exclusive video content to people who submit their answers.

Here are some survey services you can use:

- Qualaroo.com[16]

- Survey.io[17]

- SurveyMonkey.com[18]

- Typeform.com[19]

Here is a list of possible questions to ask:

- How did you find my video (brand/company) content?

- How would you feel if my videos (brand/company) no longer existed?

- What would you likely use as an alternative if my videos (brand/company) were no longer available?

- What is the primary benefit you receive from my videos (brand/company)?

- Have you recommended my videos (brand/company) to anyone?

- What type of person do you think benefits most

from my videos (brand/company)?

- How can we improve our videos (brand/company) to meet your needs?

- Is it okay if we follow-up through email if we have questions on any of your responses?

Create A Video Content Strategy

As you know, social media is all about connecting with people. The most important part about connecting with your target audience is to create content that grabs their attention.

You need to create content that resonates with the ideal customer profile you created.

Here are the types of content you can use:

- **Entertainment**: Everyone can use a good laugh during his or her day. Create something funny and share it with your audience. This can also be in the form of sports, films, or news/media.

- **Problem solving**: Create videos around a solution to a customer's problem. This is determined by their "likes" and "dislikes."

- **Q&A**: See which discussions they are taking part in and answer questions based on their most commonly asked questions.

- **Help them become more efficient**: Teach your audience something that will help them do things faster and more efficiently.

- **Newsjacking**: What is the most relevant information that relates to your target audience? What are they currently talking about? Create a video based on that.

- **Innovation**: Try to get them to tune into new ideas by recommending a service or a product to them. This should be something they didn't already know about, that you have positive experience with.

Guiding Questions

Use the following questions to help guide your video content creation strategy:

- What keywords will you target?

Use UberSuggest[20] to find the keywords you want to target in your social media efforts. These can be the keywords you use in your hashtags as well.

- Where is the value/quality of your content?

This means taking the time to really understand what your target audience wants, and deliver it to them to the best of your abilities. The quantity does not matter. As long as they enjoy consuming your content, they will keep coming back.

- How will you implement the task at hand?

Determine who will be responsible for creating the content and implementing the content strategy. Make sure you come up with a solid schedule for posting content. You also need to determine how much time and money you're willing to invest in your content.

Now we're going to go deeper into a few of the top social media networks and the tactics you should use to most effectively leverage them.

Chapter 4: How To Effectively Use The Top Social Media Sites

How To Effectively Use Google+

Google Plus[21] is an effective platform that is under-utilized by many brands.

The best part of Google+ is their Google Authorship feature, which allows your content to be indexed in search engines, instantly increasing your visibility.

The main source of traffic in this case is going to come from Google communities. This means you need to join niche communities, syndicate your content and then become the catalyst for discussions within each of them.

The most important thing to keep in mind is to join communities based on your target audience and your business niche - and then become an active contributor in these communities. If you join the wrong communities with the wrong audiences, then you will not be able to generate the quality leads you are looking for.

Whenever you have new content to post on Google Plus, make sure you link it to one of these communities. Sometimes it is relevant to tag others who have contributed to your content (use this tactic sparingly so you aren't seen as spamming).

Last of all, add a hashtag that is related to your content type and niche.

Try to get as many "+1s" on your content as you can, because this increases your visibility to your followers' audiences as well.

Best Practice: Post 3-4 times a week on Google+ and have a weekly hangout recapping all your content. This can be done in a "weekly roundup" form, so if your audience missed out during the week, then they can watch the hangout to get a recap.

How To Effectively Use Facebook For Video Promotion

The best part about Facebook[22] is that it is a learning platform. You want to use it to learn more about your target audience and their online behavior.

There are two ways to engage your audience on Facebook. The first is by using your personal profile to make connections. You, and/or your team of executives and marketers at your company must have professional Facebook profiles you use to contact prospects.

How can you use your personal Facebook profile effectively to build your video business?

1. Go to your "Friends" on Facebook.

2. On the top right, click on the "Find Friends +" feature.

3. Search for people who are local and start by building a local community before you expand your horizons.

4. Then check if the locals you connect with would be a good audience for you.

5. Hand-pick a select number of people.

6. Send them a message: "Hello this is Pattie the Pastry Chef and I just moved to _____ and I am trying to expand my network. I'd love to learn more about what there is to do around here. Could we connect?"

7. Build a relationship and connection.

8. Then send them to your videos and sell!

The second way to use Facebook is to create a business page. This will act as a central "meeting area" for all of your consumers and fans to get the newest information from you and engage with your brand.

How To Effectively Use Twitter For Video Promotion

Twitter[23] is another under-utilized tool, but it can also be the most effective tool as far as video promotion goes.

How can you promote your videos through Twitter?

With Twitter lead generation cards

Twitter Cards have been available for a while, but they have just recently become relevant to lead generation marketing. Now you are able to include opt-ins and tweet them out to your followers, for free!

You can choose the call-to-action of your choice along with a branded image. This means you can now capture their information within the Twitter platform. The best part is that you will receive their name, email address, and Twitter handle right to your inbox, for free.

To Set Up Twitter Lead Generation Cards:

1. Go to Twitter Ads and click "Creatives" and "Cards."

2. Then click on "Create Lead Generation Card."

3. Fill in the information and add an eye-catching picture. If you are sending the prospects to a landing page, fill out the destination URL.

4. Once you are done, click SUBMIT.

5. Now compose a new tweet.

6. You have the option to attach the card to your tweet in STANDARD form (FREE) or PROMOTED form ($$$).

7. "Standard" will send it out to your followers, and "Promoted" will send it to a targeted paid audience.

Best Practice: Create a lead generation card linking to free content, so your followers can learn more about who you are and what you do. This can be a whitepaper, report, eBook, or a PDF.

Followerwonk Power Tactic

FollowerWonk[24] is a tool that analyzes your Twitter followers.

1. The reason you want to use FollowerWonk is to create a Master List of your target audience.

2. This Master List is crucial in helping you find out the interests, needs and buying behavior of your target market. Once you have a Master List, start creating content around their needs, and watch your conversion rates soar!

3. Click on "Analyze" at the top, put in your Twitter handle and click submit.

4. Then download the CSV file.

5. Now click where it says "Analysis of your handle's Twitter followers" and click "view all."

6. First thing is first: delete all the followers that have no URL or destination site in their profile.

7. Next you want to filter out any social sites. Here is a list to help you: Facebook, Fb, Twitter, LinkedIn, YouTube, Instagram, Pinterest, Google, Gplus, Goo. gl, Yahoo, Amazon, Ask, Myspace, Flickr, iTunes, Vimeo, IMDB, Wikipedia, Wiki, Apple, About.me, Etsy, Flavors, Zazzle, Vizify, Soundcloud, Fiverr, Wefollow, Eventbrite, Meetup, and Forum.

8. Now go to the "Last tweet" column and find out how active your followers are. If they have not tweeted in the last 6 months, then delete them. In your excel sheet, sort them from the "oldest to newest."

9. Go to Open Site Explorer and research your current list of URLs to see who they are linked to. This will help you determine your target audience and how viable they are.

10. After completing these steps, you now have a highly targeted list of prospects you can reach out to. They have been active on Twitter, they have active sites and this leaves room for other business opportunities as well.

Best Practice: Get in touch with all your prospects through a manual, individualized email. This may sound tedious, but it is effective.

Start by sending them a "Hello, is there anything I can help you with? I see that we are both following each other on Twitter."

How To Effectively Use LinkedIn For Video Promotion

LinkedIn[25] is one platform you can't ignore. How do you

37

really promote using LinkedIn? Is it a platform that is worth your time? Yes and yes. This is one of the fastest growing social media platforms and its potentiality for your business growth is huge.

Here is how you can effectively use LinkedIn:

1. Go to the publishing platform (click on the pencil on the right of the status update on LinkedIn to publish a post).

2. Then join 50 different groups on LinkedIn that are related to your niche.

3. Participate in these groups by answering questions and asking questions.

4. The secret sauce: build a close relationship or connection with the owner of the group.

5. Message other members in the group and invite them to watch a preview of your video (make sure the video previews are targeted to their interests).

6. Click on the "Keep in touch" with contacts under the "Contacts" section and congratulate those who post about a positive life event.

Now start building your connections on LinkedIn and watch your business grow!

Chapter 5: How To Launch A Social Media Campaign

Here is a general overview of what a social media campaign looks like:

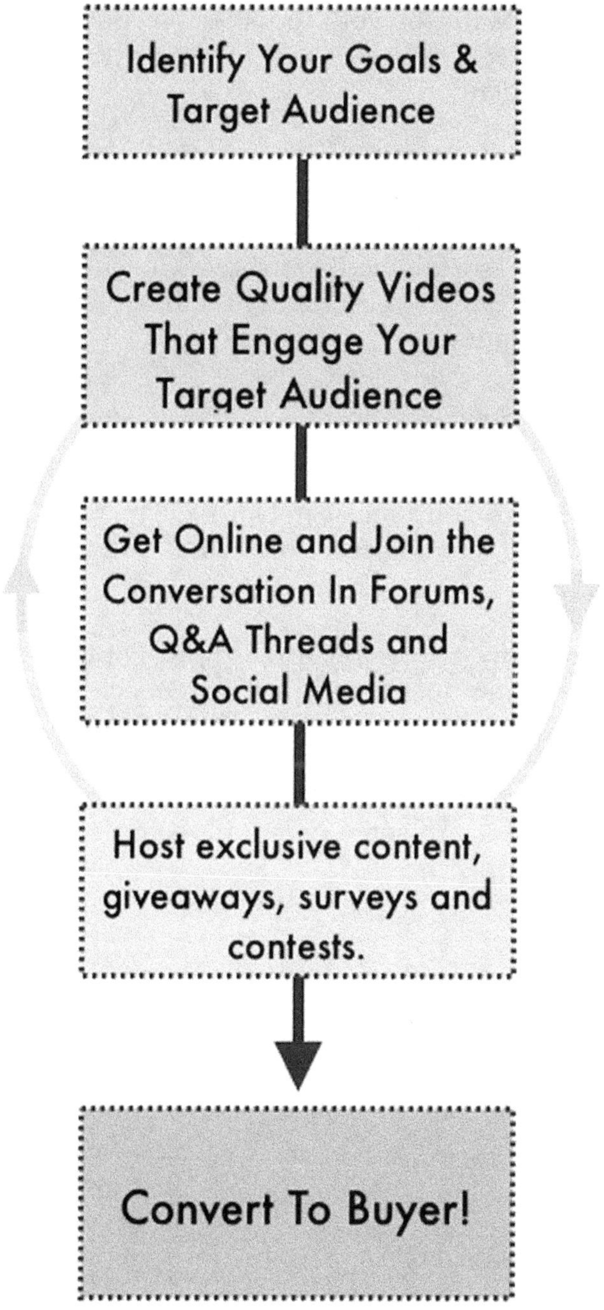

Identify Your Goals &
Target Audience

Create Quality Videos
That Engage Your
Target Audience

Get Online and Join the
Conversation In Forums,
Q&A Threads and
Social Media

Host exclusive content,
giveaways, surveys and
contests.

Convert To Buyer!

Remember to be consistent and authentic with your engagement. Many of your prospective buyers will take time to trust you and feel comfortable with buying your videos. Be patient!

Measure And Adjust

This is where you look through all your data and decide whether your social media strategy is effective or not. Remember, the plan you create is only as effective as the results you produce.

Set Up Google Analytics

First, set a baseline for all your campaigns by creating analytics for all your social networks. This way you know where you are starting from and what your plans are for growing.

There are many online resources[26] available to help you learn about how to properly set up Google Analytics on your website.

In order to track the effectiveness of your social media campaigns, here are some useful tools to use:

- Buffer[27]

- Timely[28]

- Hootsuite[29]

- TweetReach[30]

- TrendsMap[31]

- Bit.ly[32]

- Facebook Insights[33]

- Intercom[34]

Create Shortened-URLs

You want to track which campaigns are coming in from where. You will want to use Snip.ly[35] to create shortened URLs to track your social media traffic closely.

Quality Content Works Like A Charm

If you want to really attract and grab the attention of your target audience then make sure you share items that they'd be interested in. In order to benefit from your social media outreach, it is of the utmost importance to use engaging content while delivering your company's message at the same time.

Free Content

You will always want to give away a "taste" of your content. If your consumers are able to "sample" your content early on, then they will be more inclined to purchase other types of content from you.

Reel The Reviews In

When consumers watch your videos, what is the number one reason they may come back to watch it a second, third, fourth time? Would you ever watch a video again if it wasn't good the first time?

This is where value matters.

The content you create should be a combination of your passion and what your consumers want. If the consumers get what they want, then they will deliver value back to you in other forms (testimonials, social proof, and reviews).

- Ask your consumers for what they thought of the video through comments and email.

- Distribute the video on your social networks and invite your connections to view your other videos.

- Give, give, give! And then ask for a review. This means get out there and help others with your expert advice, answer questions on Q&A sites (like Quora[36] or Yahoo Answers[37]), give advice, become a leader in your industry and then ask for a review.

The other way about this is to use reviews as leverage to build a bigger consumer base.

For example, Pattie has 500 reviews on her video about making the ultimate pumpkin filled pastries. Now she doesn't have a traffic problem and she hardly ever promotes the video anymore. She gets traction to her videos through the reviews her community leave on them. Comments and reviews work like a charm to gain traffic and build a buzz around your video.

Engagement

The whole point of social media is to engage with your audience through a two-way conversation. Social networks are not made for self-promotion. Stop using social media to promote your content in an un-engaging way. Instead, use social media to start conversations and put your consumers in the spotlight.

Try featuring one of the most engaged followers on your social networks every week. This way they feel included and special, and you are able to build rapport with your audience.

Listen

When you listen to your audience you can learn and find out what they really want from you in terms of content.

This means you should use these social networks to learn and listen to your audience and their needs. The main use of the social network should be to solve your consumer's problems.

Create Conversions

Do you plan on monitoring the sales you make from your videos? Then you will have to follow a plan. Social media is the ideal medium for reaching a large number of people who are ready to buy the content you have to offer.

Most people feel as though social media doesn't convert because it requires work on both ends of your marketing funnel.

The biggest difference between social media traffic and any other traffic is that social media traffic comes with a bigger connection potential. The people who visit your site through social media will feel a connection with you.

Remember, it takes time. With consistent, high quality content delivered regularly, your audience will convert to buyers.

Additional Resources

Having a thriving online community increases your value because it becomes indisputable that your content is effective and transformative. Linking prospective customers to your online community to see for themselves what the fuss is all about will convert them to buyers.

Now that you've identified the social media networks you will be targeting with your videos, here are some additional tips and best practices to remember when using social media to boost your sales.

- Set up a support Twitter handle or Facebook Group specific to live support. You can leverage your online support group to hold weekly "live help" chats where you address popular topics in your community.

- Do one-on-one live training with those of your viewers who opt in for it. This can involve creating individualized videos just for them, or simply act as a meet and greet session. Use Google Hangouts[38] or Skype[39] as a free way to put this into practice, record the session, and then release it on your Gbox channel (how's that for making the most of your time?!).

- As an added bonus, be available to your viewers either by instant messenger or live streaming. Pattie's Pastries hosts "live cooking classes" as an added bonus to her Gbox channel. Using Google Hangouts or Skype, she engages her community by offering live cooking classes (which she also records and uploads to Gbox). You can also leverage this tactic with live tweeting. Patti live tweets with her community once a week to offer help and advice around a specific "recipe of the week."

In the next part of this book we're going to be talking about email marketing. Email marketing is one of the most effective forms of marketing when it comes to converting buyers, but it is critical that you're using it the right way. Our goal in the next section is to give you all the tools and tactics you need to create an effective email marketing campaign. Let's get started!

SECTION 3

How To Use Email
Marketing To Increase
Video Sales This Year

Email marketing plays a huge role when it comes to video content promotion. However, it is overlooked by many creators, or used ineffectively by companies resulting in a huge loss of potential profits.

Marketing online videos can be tough since it involves several different tactics and strategies. We encourage video creators to start with a marketing funnel. This funnel is comprised of a series of downloadables, surveys, email broadcasts and much more.

After we take you through the basics of email marketing, we outline all the aspects of a video selling funnel and how to implement it to drive sales to your videos.

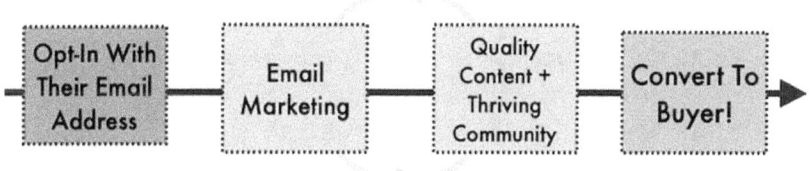

Chapter 1: Get Started With An Email Provider

There are tons of great email providers out there. How do you choose the best one? The best one is based on your preferences. For example, if you are into tech you may opt for using Infusionsoft[40]. If you are a small business then GetResponse[41] may be your best bet. We at Gbox use AWeber[42] for our email hosting, and a lot of the screenshots in this book are actual images of emails taken from our, or our featured creator's, AWeber accounts.

There are three things you want to keep in mind when choosing an email service provider.

The Ease Of Setup

You don't want use your own email to send email blasts because it may be too tedious. However, it is the best way to reach your audience without ending up in the SPAM folder. The email service provider you choose should have a seamless process when it comes to the setup. You should not have to jump through hoops. In the case that you do, then there should be a coach provided by the service to help you manage that.

If you are just starting out, we would suggest that you go with a platform that is specifically for email marketing.

Do you plan on using this for a long time? Then you want to go with something more stable, such as AWeber. However, if you decide later you want to use a platform like Infusionsoft or Salesforce[43] then know that you will have to have everyone double opt-in to your list again.

48

Deliverability

This is one of the most important aspects of email marketing. If every time you send an email it ends up in the SPAM box, then what is the point? Check the rules on the platform before you start using it. This way you can understand how to prevent your emails from hitting the SPAM folder. Most email marketing platforms have strict guidelines when it comes to uploading different lists to the platform.

All-In-One-Place

Find a platform where you are able to manage everything in one place, including analytics. Otherwise it will make it tough for you to test your campaigns. You will need to understand what is working and what isn't working. If everything is dispersed on different platforms then it may be difficult to create clear reporting and analyze your results.

Hubspot[44] is a great platform for managing everything in one place. They have landing page templates, subscriber management, and social media friendly email templates. The down side? They are relatively expensive.

Another all-in-one solution is Infusionsoft, which is not exclusively an email marketing platform, but it provides the benefits of one. Infusionsoft intertwines email with the CRM aspect giving you the benefits of both worlds

On the next pages we have put together a chart with an extensive comparison of different email service providers for you to choose from. There are a ton more, but we wanted to narrow down the list for you.

	Campaigner	MailChimp	GetResponse	iContact	AWeber
$ of Basic Plan	$19.95	$0.00	$15.00	$14.00	$19.00
Annual Plans	✗	✗	✓	✓	✗
Free Plan	✗	✓	✗	✗	✗
Free Trial	✓	✗	✓	✓	✗
Money-Back Guarantee	✗	✗	✗	✗	✓
Image Library	✓	✓	✗	✓	✗
Unlimited Emails	✓	✓	✓	✓	✓
Custom Autoresponders	✓	✓	✓	✓	✗
Email Templates	✓	✓	✓	✓	✗
Tracking	✓	✓	✓	✓	✓
Chat Spport	✓	✗	✓	✓	✓
24/7 Phone Support	✓	✗	✗	✗	✗
Multiple Users	✓	✗	✓	✗	✗
Gmail Import	✓	✓	✓	✗	✗
Sign-Up Forms	✓	✓	✓	✓	✓
Google Analytics	✓	✓	✓	✗	✗
User Segments	✓	✗	✓	✓	✓
Survey	✗	✗	✓	✓	✗
A/B Testing	✓	✓	✓	✗	✓
Social Media Marketing	✓	✗	✓	✓	✗

The next step is to find a basic email template in order to send out consistent-looking emails to your subscriber list. Don't worry, you don't need to learn programming or send out HTML emails. We recommend using a very basic email template with your logo, your contact information, and your brand colors.

	Benchmark Email	Campaign Monitor	Constant Contact	Vertical Response	GraphicMail
$ of Basic Plan	$11.95	$9.00	$20	$0.00	$9.95
Annual Plans	✓	✗	✗	✗	✗
Free Plan	✓	✗	✗	✓	✗
Free Trial	✗	✓	✓	✗	✗
Money-Back Guarantee	✗	✓	✓	✗	✗
Image Library	✓	✗	✓	✓	✓
Unlimited Emails	✓	✗	✓	✓	✓
Custom Autoresponders	✓	✓	✗	✗	✓
Email Templates	✓	✓	✓	✓	✓
Tracking	✓	✓	✓	✓	✓
Chat Spport	✓	✗	✓	✓	✓
24/7 Phone Support	✗	✗	✗	✗	✗
Multiple Users	✗	✓	✗	✗	✗
Gmail Import	✗	✗	✓	✗	✓
Sign-Up Forms	✓	✓	✓	✓	✓
Google Analytics	✓	✓	✓	✗	✓
User Segments	✓	✓	✓	✓	✓
Survey	✓	✗	✓	✗	✗
A/B Testing	✓	✓	✗	✗	✗
Social Media Marketing	✓	✓	✗	✗	✓

Here are three sources you can use to find email templates:

Themeforest[45] has some great templates that are affordable. The chances of not finding what you need here is slim.

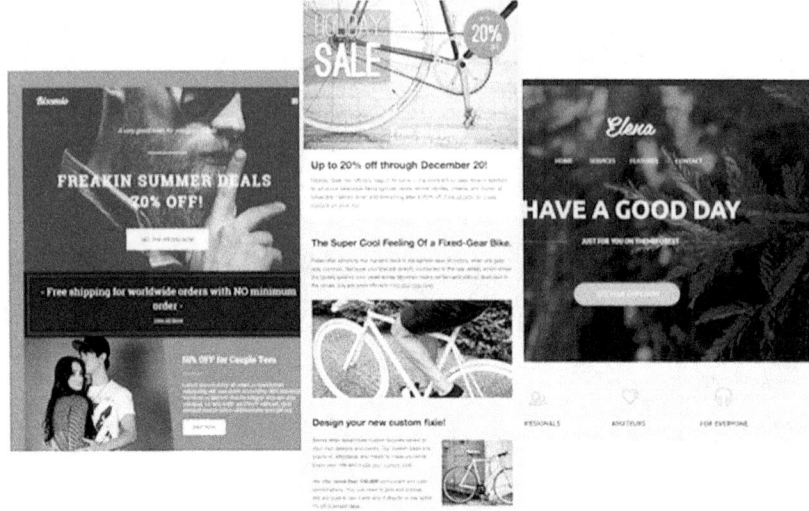

Campaign Monitor[46] is known for bringing together some of the world's best designers and releasing hundreds of free templates. These are smooth, simple and professional at the same time. If you are looking for a layout that meets your needs, this is the place to find it.

Templateria[47] has some professional looking templates if you are going for sophistication and class. These templates have been used for years and the designs are completely unique.

Once you have these two things in place you are ready to start increasing your subscriber base!

How To Build Your Database Of Consumers

Building an audience isn't something that happens overnight. The secret formula is having a full understanding of your subscribers. When you know who they are (your ideal client), then finding them and creating a message that speaks to them is feasible.

Take a moment to write down what your goals are for your audience. What do you want to achieve with them?

What type of customer are you aiming for? Here are the three most common groups:

Greenfield & Free Trial Customers: This is when your customer experience matters most. These customers are engaging with your video content for the first time and they aren't loyal customers just yet.

Regular Customers: These are customers who come

back to you over and over again. They are in the same realm as loyal customers. They love what you have to offer!

Readers: These are usually blog subscribers. People who are interested in written information and educational resources. They are on the hunt for finding information but they are not your customers yet. They aren't even interested in your marketing or what you have to offer.

When it comes to gaining traction and building a subscriber base, start with a seed list first. This means you get the customer's email address through a transaction, sign-up or checkout. If you know your target customer, then you can easily create trigger-events to send them newsletters and email blasts as often as they want them.

Here are some ways to collect email addresses:

Personalize Your Call-To-Action

When you create call-to-actions such as "Submit now" or "Click here", they are not as personalized as "I want to learn how to make more money with email marketing now!" These long-form call-to-actions have a lot to do with the responsiveness of the campaign. When you create an ethical bribe, make sure the call-to-action stands out. In a call-to-action button or call-out box, the most common colors to use are yellow and orange.

Here are some examples of high-impact call-to-action buttons:

LIKE Ꮐ boxON FACEBOOK

Hey Hull FC Follower!

We want to know more about you

CLICK HERE

to fill out a 1-minute survey

And we'll send you a free gift!

HULL F.C.

 CLICK HERE **for Paul the Personal Trainer's Step-by-Step Process!**

Surveys Say It All

We prefer using Qualaroo[48] to create simple surveys all throughout our website. This way we are able to capture the preferences that matter most to our creators.

You should implement the same when it comes to the consumers on your website or video channel. The data you receive from your consumers will help you plan and create content they want to see and pay for. The more it is catered to their needs, the better the chance of retaining the consumer.

Simple questions may include:

- What are you expecting to receive from our content?
- Is this page easy to understand?
- What topics are you interested in?
- How often do you want to receive updates from us?

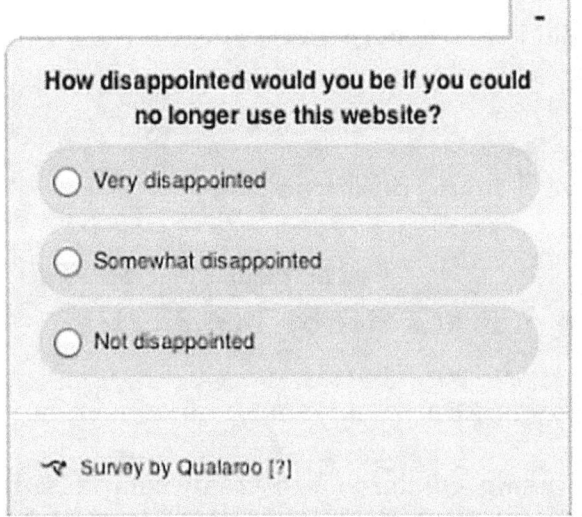

In fact, you can even ask them if they want to receive consistent updates from you by using this survey:

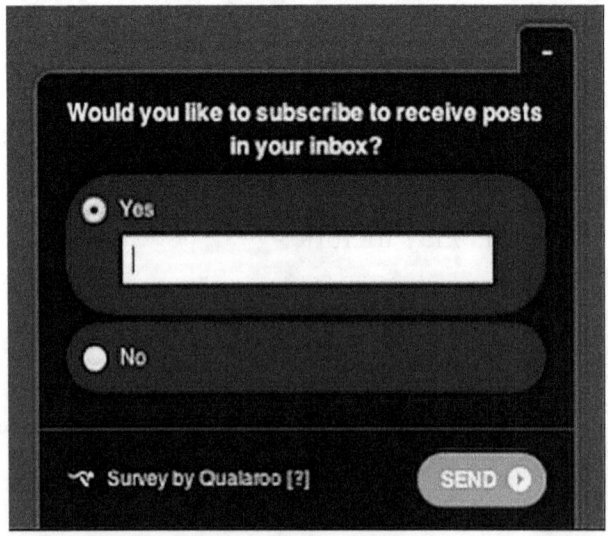

Exit Pops Work Like A Charm

First determine which pages on your website are receiving the most traffic. Those are the pages you will want to add an exit pop to. Usually exit pops are placed on the homepage of the site. This is because when your brand is Googled, your consumers will land on that page first. The premise behind the exit pop is to capture names and email addresses. These pop ups can give away case studies, templates, and other types of exclusive content your consumer has not been able to find before. There is so much you can do with an email address you would be surprised. Imagine being able to sell consistently just by blasting an email! This is the type of revenue stream we want to help you build. Well, here are examples of some of the best exit pops in town:

Andrew Chen[49] uses something called "full-page interstitial popups" so their consumers are not frustrated when they come to their site and don't see their blog there. This will ensure more subscribes and consumers. This helps you be more laser-focused on their needs.

@andrewchen

Join 90,000+ people who get my tech newsletter – it features long-form essays on what's going on here in Silicon Valley.

I've written 550+ essays which have been featured and quoted in The New York Times, Fortune, Wired, and WSJ. The topics range from mobile product design to fundraising to "growth hacking."

email@domain.com

Get new essays by email

 Here's one message you want. Chen's weekly newsletter offers thoughtful essays on startups and marketing from a true Silicon Valley insider.

– *Wired Magazine*

Laser-Focused Destinations

Now that we have the basics down when it comes to capturing subscribers, lets move onto creating landing pages that will impact whether someone may opt-in to your list or not.

Have you ever clicked on an ad online and were taken to a webpage that asked you to take action (such as take a survey, enter an email address, fill out a form, etc.)? If you have, then you've seen a landing page already. As you capture leads, you want to funnel them into one place where you can manage them, and that is where the landing page comes in.

We use a combination of LeadPages[50] and AWeber to create a sign-up form within the site. LeadPages has A/B testing tools, which allows you to test what is working and what isn't when it comes to converting on your landing pages. Start with 3 different landing page designs and see which one converts the best. Then keep the one that is converting for all of your campaigns.

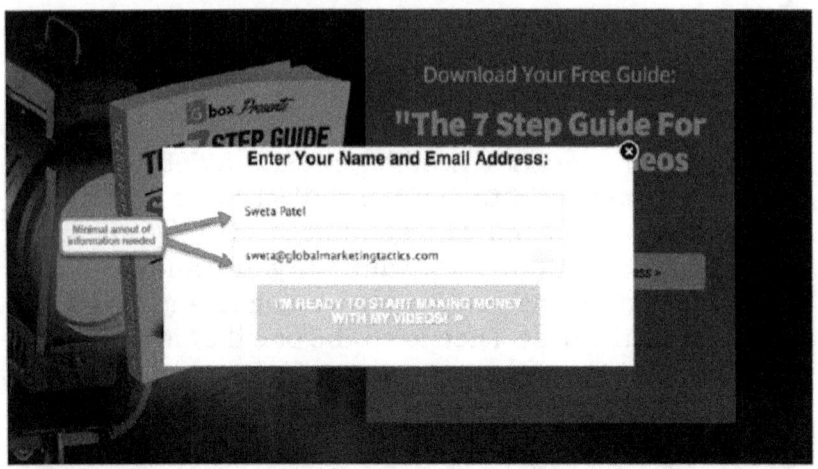

Then we create a list in AWeber to complement the sign-up form.

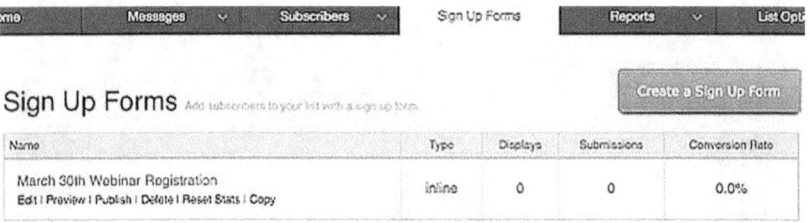

Once these things are done, then we head over to LeadPages and integrate the AWeber form with our designated landing page.

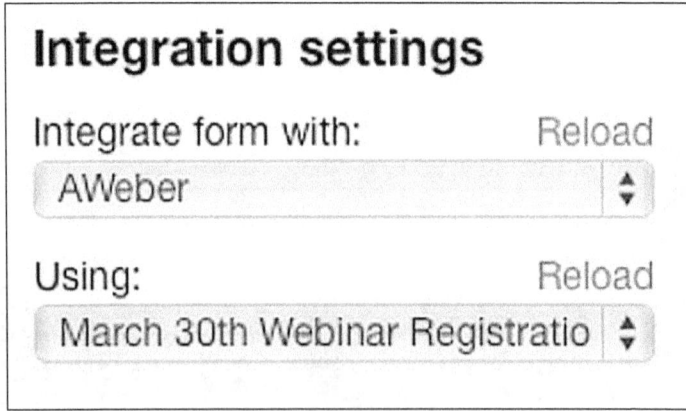

When it comes to designing your landing pages, the design must be minimalistic, simple, and catchy to the eyes. One large image is usually enough to capture someone's attention. Less is more when it comes to content on the landing page. We usually have 12-15 words on our landing pages. We use the copy to showcase our brand. The message should not lose its context and form. Examples of great landing pages that have converted in the past:

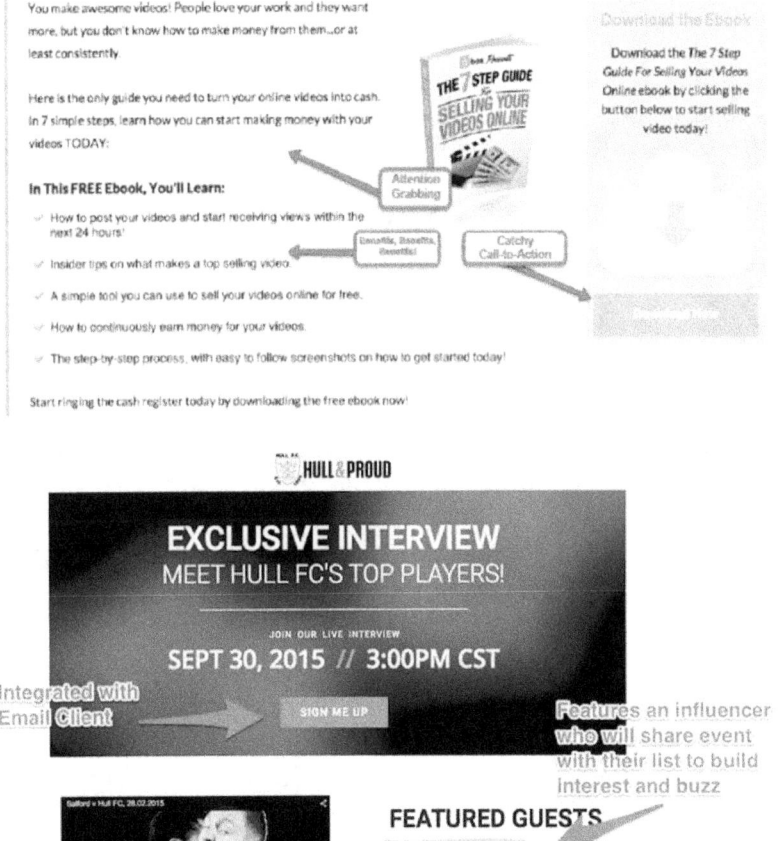

In fact, you can even add an opt-in form on the side of the blog page of your website or all throughout your site. We use SumoMe[51] to implement this on our blog. We want to make sure we never miss out on a chance to get someone's email address added to our list.

You should link to your landing page from these different areas: blog sidebar, header of your homepage, and your social media channels.

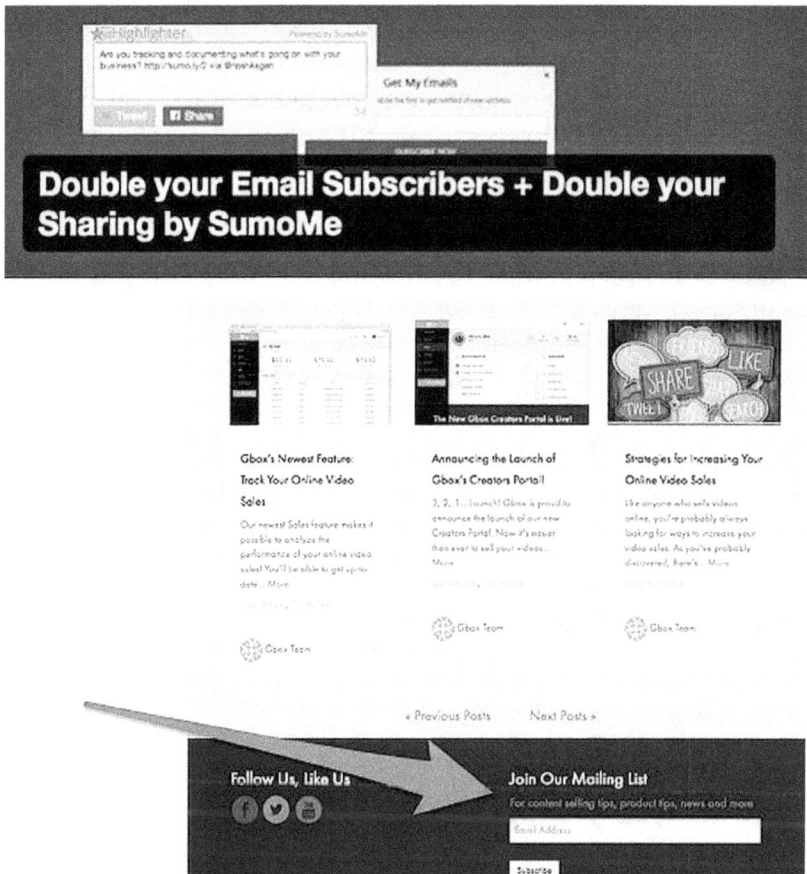

Now that you have a way to capture email addresses, now it's time to set up your email newsletter.

Automated Campaigns vs. Single Blasts

What do you think of when you think of email marketing? The first thing that may come to your mind is an "email newsletter." Even though email newsletters have been around since the 1990's, businesses are getting savvier with how they use them. They are now using a lifecycle marketing approach. You can't just use basic segmentation and blast it out to your list anymore.

You want to use email marketing for three reasons: to build your consumer loyalty, for consumer retention, and to increase your video sales and engagement. Creating an email sequence is one thing, but actually nurturing the community and the list is another.

What happens when you do something once and never do it again? People tend to forget about it. What are you going to do so your videos are on the top of their mind?

Here are the two types of campaigns:

Newsletter or Email Blasts: This is focused on the more traditional approach where you send an update email once a day, once a week or once a month.

Follow Up Series An automated series of emails sent to new subscribers.

Drag and drop messages to change their order.

#1	[ACCESS] Your 7 Step Guide For Selling Your... Edit I Send a test I Delete I Copy		Send immediately
#2	Online Videos are 2015's Big Money-Maker Edit I Send a test I Delete I Copy	M-F 6AM-9AM	Send 1 day after the previous message
#3	Want to create an irresistible movement? Edit I Send a test I Delete I Copy	M-F 6AM-9AM	Send 1 day after the previous message
#4	5-minute hack for selling videos online Edit I Send a test I Delete I Copy	M-F 6AM-9AM	Send 1 day after the previous message
#5	How to build an online video empire Edit I Send a test I Delete I Copy	M-F 6AM-9AM	Send 1 day after the previous message

Automated Campaigns: You can trigger these campaigns through a certain type of customer behavior. We use Customer.io[52] to trigger these events and campaigns. For example, if someone comes to your website and doesn't buy, or if someone watches your video and they don't come back.

Spend some time with the copy on both of these campaigns to maximize the conversion rates on your videos.

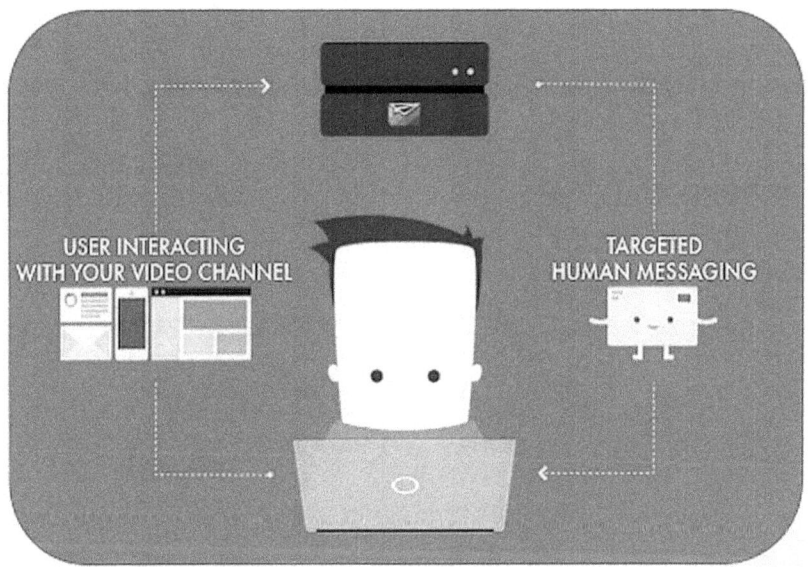

The Automated Campaign Flow

Let's think about your video sales funnel from end-to-end.

What are the exact steps for taking the customer from a landing page or your website, to the actual conversion? Once you create your funnel, determine how email marketing will help move your consumers from Point A to Point B in the funnel.

Here is a typical funnel for selling online videos:

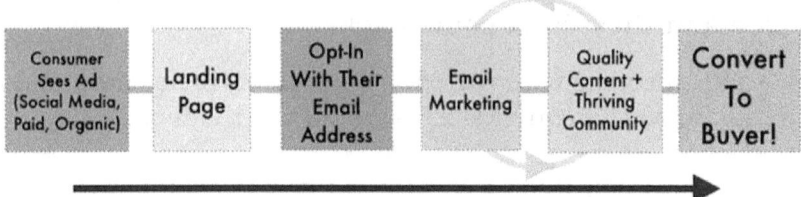

Here is how you can infuse email marketing into your funnel flow:

1. Email consumers who come to your landing page and don't buy from you.

2. Email consumers when they come to your landing page and they don't opt-in for what you are selling. You can also retarget them with different content and send them an email.

3. Email consumers who click "buy" but don't complete the purchase.

HULL F.C.

HULL & PROUD

EST. 1865

Hey there Hull FC SuperFan!

Our last match against the Wigan Warriors was INSANE!

We know you don't want to miss out on all the action, which is why we'd love to offer you a discounted season's pass.

That's right!

You're a valued fan, and we don't want you to miss one single game.

Click below to get a FREE preview of our last game - which includes EXCLUSIVE interviews of our starting line-up, PLUS an in-depth report on our predictions for the rest of the season.

Click below to watch!

James Ray
Hull FC Fan Club Manager

First Call-To-Action

Second Call-To-Action

Exclusive video content that links to your main video channel

The next thing you want to do is to create a worksheet behind the basic ideas of your email marketing campaign:

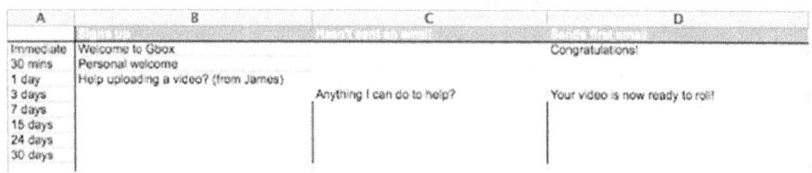

A	B	C	D
	Signs up	Hasn't sent an email	Sends first email
Immediate	Welcome to Gbox		Congratulations!
30 mins	Personal welcome		
1 day	Help uploading a video? (from James)		
3 days		Anything I can do to help?	Your video is now ready to roll!
7 days			
15 days			
24 days			
30 days			

This should give you a good idea of the goal of each email you send out.

Remember to list out your desired goals for conversion! Everything in your funnel and email marketing needs to link back to your outcomes.

The Educational Email Campaign

The idea of this campaign is to turn subscribers into video consumers. We can accomplish this through a series of 5-8 emails within a 30-day period.

Here are some examples of what it looks like:

Step 1: Welcome Email/Thanks for subscribing. It should give them the inside scoop on what they will be receiving from you.

Step 2: Informs them about the problem and gives them a little more background about how they can solve their frustrations with the problem.

Step 3: Send them a few training teasers that show them you are the expert at what you do.

Create curiosity to hook the reader in.

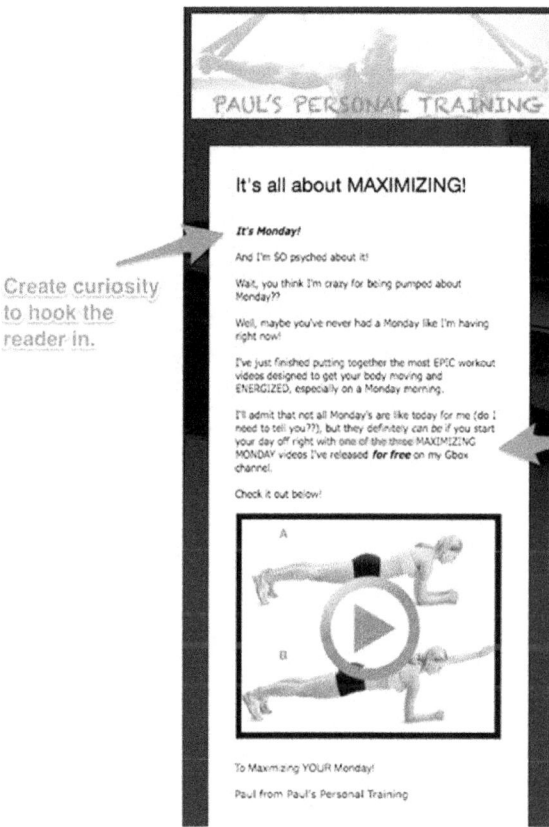

Paul always creates more than one free video to be released at a time to maximize the chance of his viewers finding something that suits them.

Step 4: Offer a solution to the problem from a different angle. This is when you first introduce what you are selling.

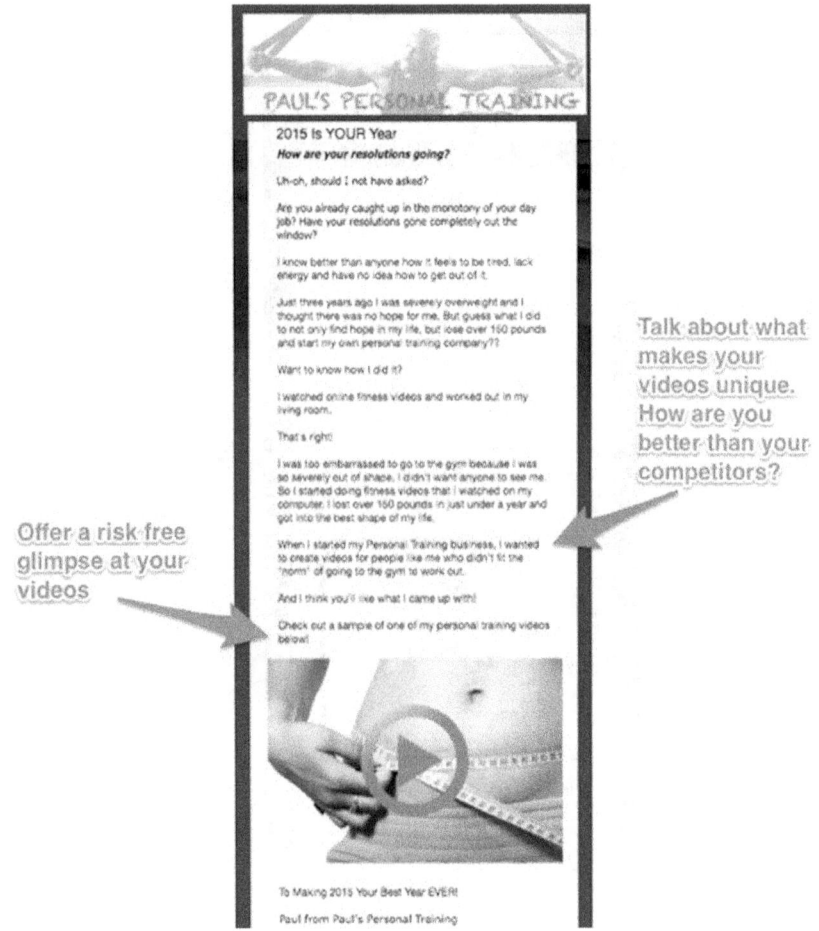

Step 5: Describe their situation or problem better than they can. Go deeper into the problem solving aspect and figuring out their issue.

Make it
personal - Pull
at the
heartstrings!

Today I wanted to reach out to talk about overcoming the odds.

I know that it's not just about working out.

It's deeper than that.

You want to gain confidence. You want your friends and family members to value you and benefit from your healthy habits.

You want to be able to live a long, full life.

And it's not just about knowing *where or how* to start changing your life. Maybe you lack the faith that you're even *able* to start.

I know how you feel because I've been there.

Last week I told you about how just three years ago I was severely overweight and had given up on myself.

I know, just like you do, that there's more to it than just exercising. There are also psychological and emotional factors deeply ingrained in us that make it harder than most people to exercise.

That's why I'm so confident that you will benefit from watching the video I've put together below.

In it I talk about my personal story and struggle, and what I did (and still do today!) to overcome some huge obstacles in my life. Learn how I lost over 100 pounds in less than a year, and what I do today to keep the pounds off.

I know you're really going to enjoy it.

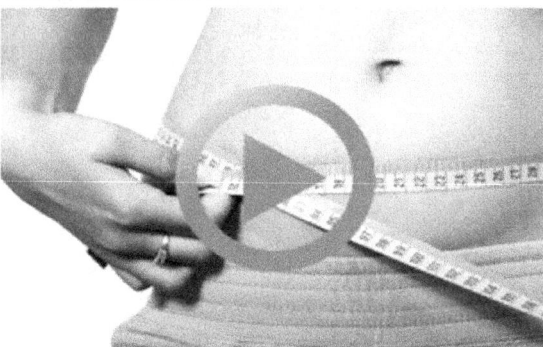

To understand and overcoming.

From, Paul of Paul's Personal Training

Step 6: Give away your top stuff! Yes give them things they can actually use and benefit from.

Step 7: End the campaign and offer a low-priced deal for your videos.

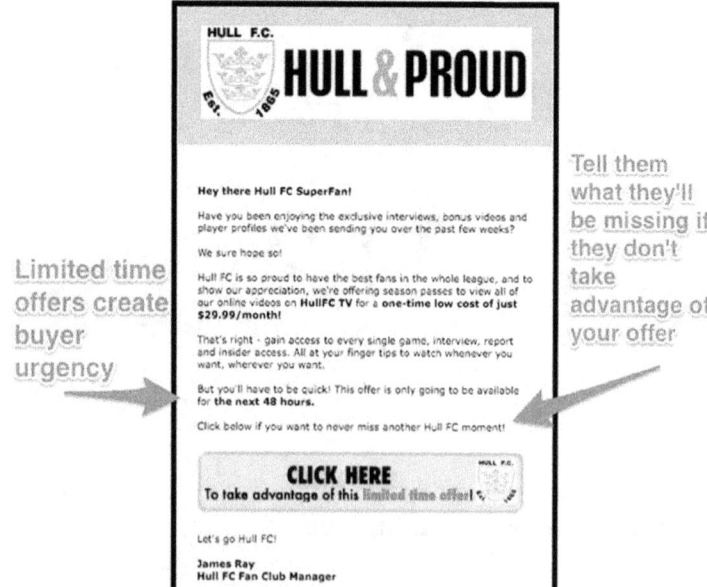

All your emails should have large CTA (Call-to-action) buttons in them.

ENTER TO WIN!
Your Own Personal Training Video!

CLICK HERE
To take advantage of this
limited time offer!

You can automate this campaign and use it over and over again with these various groups:

• Target new subscribers.

• Use it for your landing pages.

• If you have a video offer, then you can implement it on the exit pop of your home page.

• You can target customers who watch your videos but don't purchase from you.

In order to keep your subscribers coming back, you must have amazing content in your emails. Let's get into that next.

How To Create AMAZING Content

You have to demonstrate value every time you send your subscribers an email.

Subject Lines

The first thing your subscribers will notice is your subject line. Sometimes we spend 30-40 minutes just crafting our subject line. Studies say you should allocate 80% of your time crafting the subject line. Imagine if you create the most amazing email but your subscribers don't even open it? If they don't open it then you won't be able to get them to click and convert.

Check this out: Today's subject line doesn't just consist of the "subject line." The new subject line includes the subject line, the "from address" and even the first few lines of the email.

This gives you more real estate to work with in terms of getting your subscribers to open your emails.

Here are some things to consider when crafting your subject line:

- Never just leave your brand name in the subject.

- Put in the 'from' name. For example, "Sweta from Gbox."

- Make sure the first few lines of your email content count.

Here are a few quick tips to infuse in your subject lines:

Generate Fear, Curiosity, or Scarcity

All of these emotions will get customers to open the email. You can start the subject line with a question that shows them what they will be missing out on if they don't open the email. Include items that could possibly double or triple the amount of something they can relate to.

Here are some examples:

EXAMPLE 1:

Subject: We bet you won't open this email...

Headline: Hey, you opened the email! How's that for some reverse psychology?

Body: Today I'm going to give you my top 10 marketing tips on how to use reverse psychology to triple your leads.

EXAMPLE 2:

Subject: Are you CRAZY?

Headline: Maybe you aren't, but I definitely am!

Body: Don't tell my boss, because what I'm about to tell you is completely NUTS. For the next 24 hours only I want to give you unlimited access to ALL of our best selling videos for less than $10.

Data To Improve Your Results

This may be a bit difficult, but don't just use your subscriber's name. You want to use information that you know about them to personalize the email. This may take some time to collect, but the effort goes far to convert! For example, LinkedIn sends a personalized email with who has viewed your LinkedIn profile.

Hey there, Paul here from Paul's Personal Training.

On your profile it says you've lost over 20 pounds using my fitness videos!

Laura in my personal training community reached out to me because she saw your profile and she's really interested in finding out more about what videos you've been following.

I'd love to connect the two of you. Are you interested?

Let me know!

Paul from Paul's Personal Training

Link Series Emails Together

If you are creating an "orientation" similar to what GetResponse[53] does with their email marketing tutorials, then you want to group them together. You will want to add: Chapter 1, Chapter 2, Chapter 3 and so on. This will prompt the reader to anticipate the next email.

MORE EXAMPLES:

Email 1 subject line: "Your month of personalized training videos starts here!"

Email 2 subject line: "Week one: Arm toning exercises using household items"

Email 3 subject line: "Week two: Customized squat variations just for you"

The Types Of Content That Actually Work

The secret to creating content that actually engages and converts is one word: *education.* You want to create content that educates the consumer to the buying process of your videos. It is not about the discounts and the cheap offers. Your emails should be about sharing your knowledge about what you hope they can gain from it.

When you start delivering value, people will look over the simple grammar and spelling mistakes you make. These won't matter because you are providing them with great content they can benefit from.

Everyone tends to move towards the best or the person who is the best at what they do. If this is your passion, then work on becoming the best at it. Practice everyday, because consumers will gravitate towards top-notch videos in the industry. If you are not there yet, then be very upfront and honest. This will help you relate to your community because they will appreciate the transparency. If consumers can't relate to you, then you will have a hard time selling.

Who Should The Email Be From?

We always use "Sweta from Gbox" as our 'from' address. The point of this portion of the email is to make your consumers aware of who they are receiving the email from. You don't want to leave them in the dark or question who the email is from. If they have to question who it is from then it will most likely get deleted fast.

From our own studies at Gbox, we realized never to use cases like this:

- noreply@gbox.com   • Sweta@gbox.com
- Gbox   • Sweta Patel

They should know who you are and where the email is coming from, which is why we use "Sweta from Gbox."

To Your Video Empire Success,
Sweta from Gbox
Marketing Guru
sweta@gbox.com

Paul of Paul's Personal Training
Fitness Fanatic
paul@personaltraining.com

The Power Of The Call-To-Action

The CTA has a huge impact on the success of your email marketing campaign. You want to be sure you only have one action per webpage/email. Here is what you want to keep in mind when it comes to the CTA of your campaign:

Consistency

This is where what you are asking the customer to do is consistent with the subject line and the body of your email.

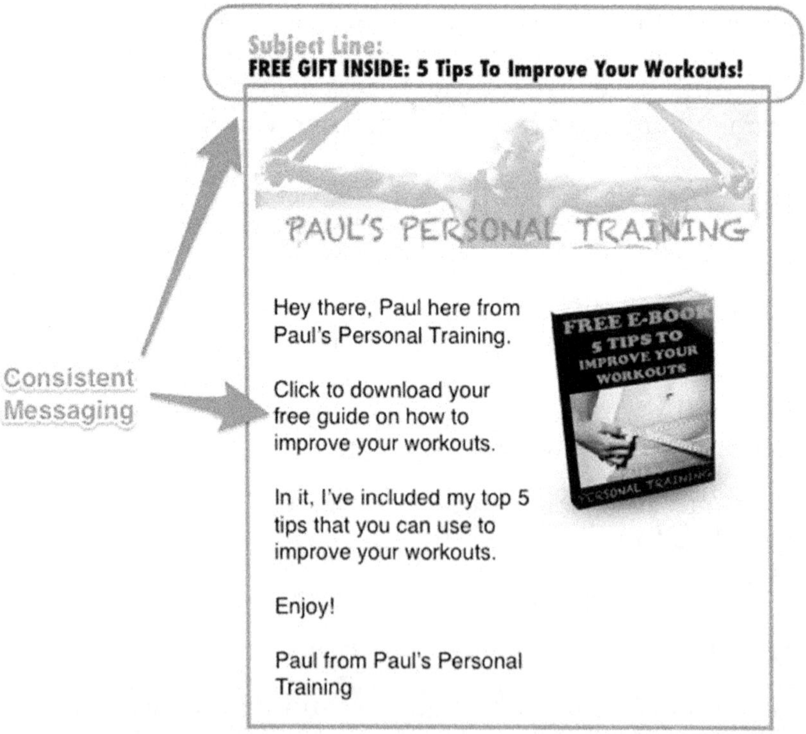

Subject Line:
FREE GIFT INSIDE: 5 Tips To Improve Your Workouts!

PAUL'S PERSONAL TRAINING

Hey there, Paul here from Paul's Personal Training.

Click to download your free guide on how to improve your workouts.

In it, I've included my top 5 tips that you can use to improve your workouts.

Enjoy!

Paul from Paul's Personal Training

FREE E-BOOK
5 TIPS TO
IMPROVE YOUR
WORKOUTS

Consistent
Messaging

Relevant & Relatable

Be sure your emails are relatable to the person you are sending them out to. They should not feel as though they cannot relate to anything you send in the email. They should be anticipating your emails.

Action

What are you asking them to do? How will it improve their life 100%? Or even make their life easier? Remember to always format the email so that the reader can take action directly in the email instead of having to click through to a separate site.

Targeted

Your emails must be targeted to the right audience. If your emails are not segmented in your email client, then this will have a huge effect on who opens your emails and who doesn't. If they say something like, "what does this have to do with me?" then you are making them do too much work and your emails have a strong chance of getting deleted.

HULL F.C.

HULL & PROUD

Hey there Hull FC SuperFan!

We played the York City Knights last night and boy, was it a great game.

We see that you didn't catch the replay on our Hull FC Live Channel - if you'd like to watch, click below to get all play-by-play action.

Watch Now On The Hull FC Live Channel!   HULL F.C.

You can also catch all our latest videos including match re-caps and the latest analysis from the coaches.

We can't wait for you to see all the exclusive content.

James Ray
Hull FC Fan Club Manager

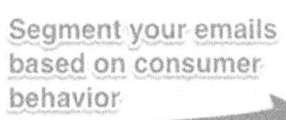

Segment your emails based on consumer behavior

How To Nurture Your Database

Are all your subscribers receiving the same information from you over and over again? It is time to change it up and send out more relevant information to your consumers.

Segment Your Consumers

You can segment your consumers vertically by industry or horizontally by their preferences. This will allow you to group the emails you send and track your results. Not to mention it will keep your subscribers around longer. You want to start thinking about segmenting your subscribers the moment they opt-in to any of your landing pages.

Highly segmented lists make it easy to cater your content to specific viewers

Email Marketing & Analytics

Current In-House Clients **All current personal training clients**	Active	646 Subscribers
Season Pass Subscribers **Current subscribers of video season passes**	Active	279 Subscribers
Twitter Referrals **Prospects found via Twitter**	Active	995 Subscribers
Facebook Referrals **Prospects found via Facebook**	Active	827 Subscribers

Here are the three most common ways to segment your subscribers:

Consumer Attributes

You can target consumers through specific details such as age, gender, the number of purchases they have made, or where they are geographically located. As you build relationships with your customers you will need to learn more about them. This will allow you to segment them more feasibly.

You can create call to actions within your landing pages to learn more about your customers and what they do.

Their Online Behavior

This is where you will have to keep track of what the customer has bought from you and what they haven't bought from you. From this information you can create more targeted emails. For example, when they go to your website and don't buy a video from you several times then you can track this and send them a laser-focused email.

Social Interests & Interactions

Social data can help you segment your audience based on their preferences and their interactions with you on channels such as Facebook and Twitter. For example, if I was speaking to Johnny on Twitter and I saw that he enjoyed outdoor adventures, I would add him to my Twitter list within AWeber, and tag him with a keyword such as "outdoors." This way I know who I met where and what their preferences were. When it comes around to Johnny's birthday I can send him a gift certificate to watch my Safari adventure video. Now that is hyper-personalized!

The Opting-Out Process

According to CAN-SPAM rules and regulations you must follow these guidelines:

1. Include an unsubscribe link in all of your marketing emails and honor unsubscribe requests within 10 days.

2. The 'from' addresses, names and subject lines must be relevant and not misleading.

3. The physical address of the sender must also be included in all emails you send.

4. You must ask for permission before sending out emails to your consumers.

The penalties for not following these rules can cost you thousands.

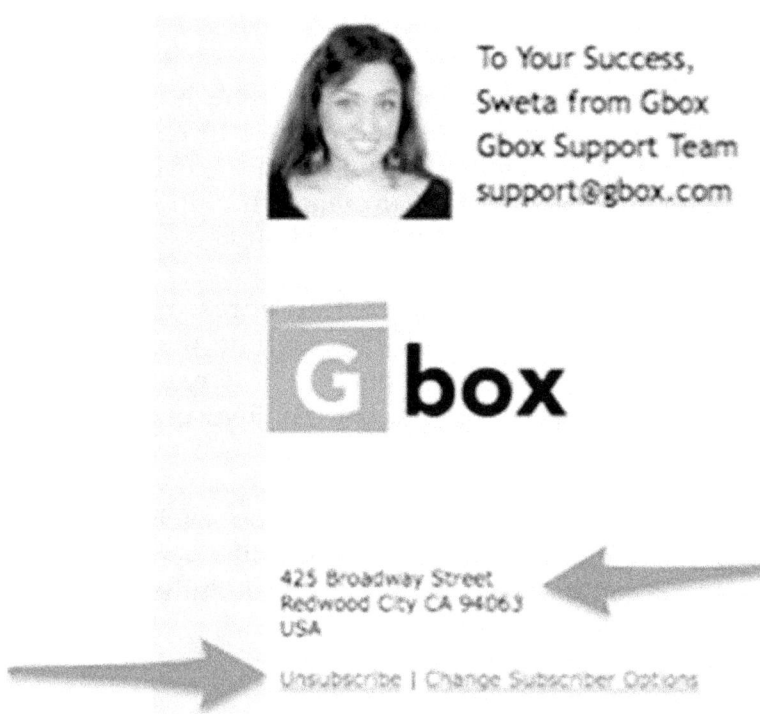

The best approach to this is to unsubscribe people on your list automatically if they have not interacted with you for a certain period of time. For example, if they have not engaged with any of your campaigns in 30 days then you should send them an email telling them that you have opted them out.

Email Send Out Times

We always get asked when the best time is to send out emails. Data has been collected on this to show that the best time to send emails is (possibly) in the early morning. Why? Most people check their email when they first wake up in the morning while they are still in bed.

That being said, despite the amount of research that has been done, MailChimp[54] concludes that there may not actually be an ideal time to send out an email. They came to this conclusion after sending out millions of emails every week.

At the end of the day, it depends on each individual customer. What is the average day like for your ideal customer? You have to know your target audience!

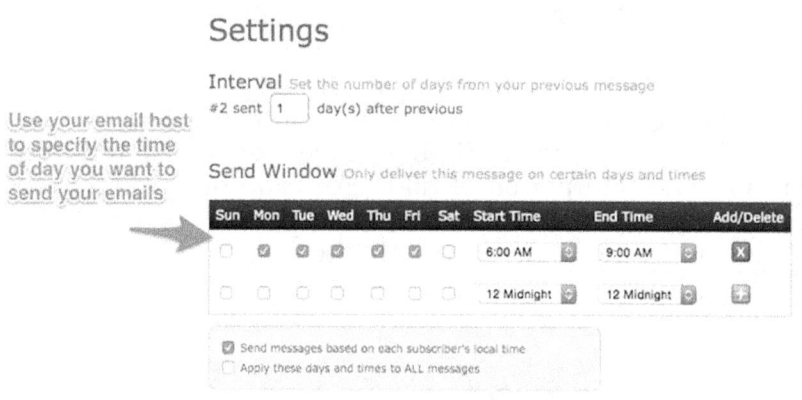

Chapter 2: Launch & Measure Your Results

How can you improve something that isn't being measured? Now that you have a solid foundation of setting up your email campaigns to your specific audiences, it is time to start making your campaigns live.

Make sure you have an email blast campaign and an automated campaign running at the same time. When these two campaigns are running, you should see consistent improvements in your marketing figures. Just make sure you measure everything.

Here are the metrics you need to measure when it comes to your email marketing campaigns:

Opens

Depending on your email hosting service, your email open rates are tracked automatically. Sometimes open rates are underreported because images have been disabled by 60% of your reader's email clients. This is a default setting and you may not have control over this.

Subject: We bet you won't open this email...

Sent to 3,402 subscribers at 03/17/15 18:00 PM

1302 390
opened clicked

Clicks

Unique clicks let you know how many people have engaged with your email. The total number of clicks shows how many times a consumer opens an email.

This is an important metric to measure in the long-term. However, if a consumer opens an email and forwards it to four of his friends, then the total clicks would only show one recipient, meaning all the opens are connected to one person.

See how the total number of clicks can get a bit messy?

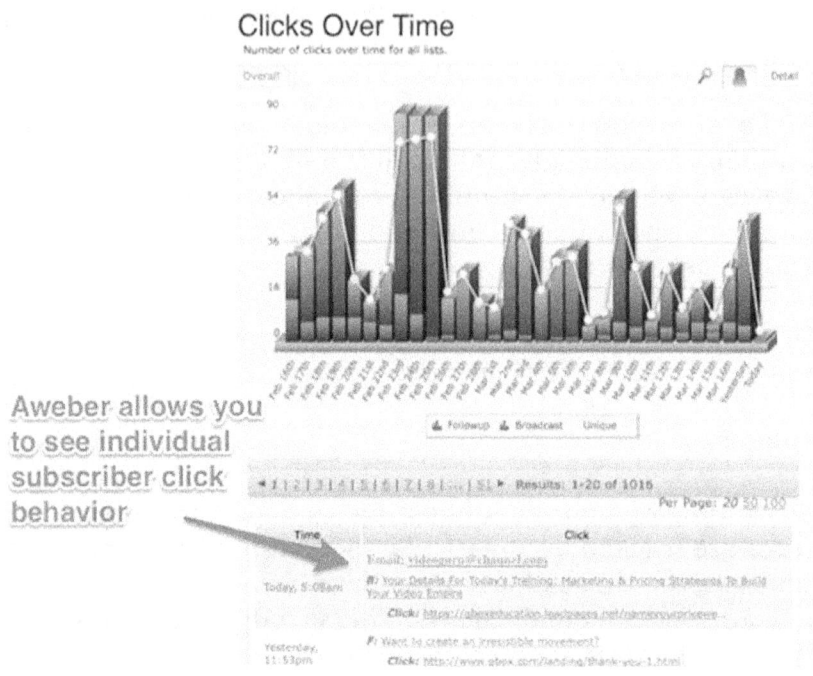

Which Metric Is Most Relevant To You And Your Business?

Conversions

Tracking conversions is the toughest element to test. Make sure you tag all the links in your outgoing email campaigns with Google UTM tags[55].

This will allow you to track conversions in Google Analytics. After you create all the tags, then go back and create goals for your campaigns.

For example, you can create a goal for a specific email campaign. This will allow you to track which customers came from which campaigns.

URL builder

Use this tool to add Custom Campaign parameters to your URLs.

The URL builder helps you add parameters to URLs you use in Custom Campaigns. When users click one of the custom links, the unique parameters are sent to your Google Analytics account, so you can identify the URLs that are most effective in attracting users to your content.

Using the URL builder

Fill in the form below and click **Submit** button to create URLs for Custom Campaigns for website tracking.

Use the Google Play URL builder tool ☑ for mobile app tracking.

When you enter your URL, you need to *escape* special characters. For example, if your URL contains a string like topic=1638563&rd=1, you need to *escape* the ampersand, and enter that portion of the URL like this: topic=1638563&rd=1

Step 1: Enter the URL of your website.

Website URL *

(e.g. http://www.urchin.com/download.html)

Step 2: Fill in the fields below. **Campaign Source, Campaign Medium and Campaign Name** should always be used.

Campaign Source *

(referrer: google, citysearch, newsletter4)

Campaign Medium *

(marketing medium: cpc, banner, email)

Campaign Term

(identify the paid keywords)

Campaign Content

(use to differentiate ads)

Campaign Name *

(product, promo code, or slogan)

SUBMIT   * Required field

Specify Each Channel Using A UTM Code

If this is not already set up within your email marketing platform, you'll want to use Google Analytics to track where your traffic is coming from by using UTM codes in all your URLS.

Use UTM codes to track your conversion rates. Think about it: would you like to see 40 clicks and 35 conversions, or 2000 clicks and 2 conversions? Just don't forget to track your goals!

Here are some possible hypotheses you can use to help determine what is not working with your email campaigns.

- Are they not opening the emails because the subject line is not catchy or compelling enough?

- Do your customers know what action to take next? Is your CTA not clear enough or is it confusing?

- Are your emails getting ignored because you are emailing way too much?

- Do they open the email but fail to click because of other distractions?

- Is your landing page not relevant to the email? So when they click through they aren't receiving what they expected?

In just a few pages we talk about the power of A/B Testing and how you can use it to identify problems with your email campaign, and then solve them!

Google Analytics Multi-Channel Attribution

Imagine if a consumer finds your website on Google through an ad that was re-marketed to them via Facebook - then they were sent an automated email for viewing a preview of your video, and then leaving your site.

What triggered the conversion? This is why it is important to set up the multi-channel attribution within Google Analytics. Otherwise the conversion will be determined from the consumer's last direct interaction.

With multi-channel attribution, you can actually assign special channel grouping.

Here is what it should look like:

View & Analyze Your Results Within Google Analytics

Now you can measure how effective your campaigns are. This will allow you to save money on your campaigns and help them to convert better.

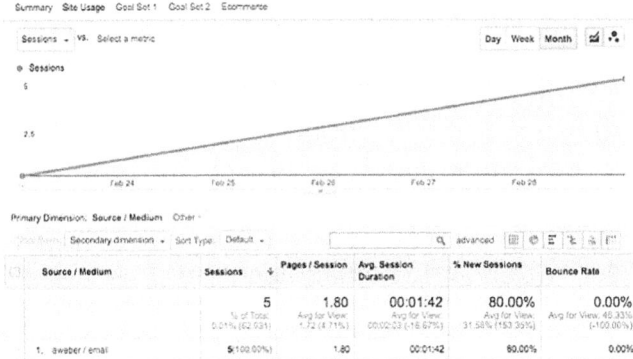

Chapter 3: The Power Of A/B Testing

Literally every email you send is the opportunity to get valuable feedback on how to improve your conversion rates.

If you're sending out emails and crossing your fingers hoping they'll get opened and have sky-high conversion rates, you're leaving a lot up to chance. Ask yourself this: how do you expect to improve your conversion rates if you have no information about why your audience is opening (or not opening) your emails in the first place?

We've got good news. You can start getting feedback from your existing list on their email opening and reading behavior with just a few minor tweaks to how you're already sending out emails. Follow these steps to learn how you can use the information you get to drastically improve your email campaigns and increase your video sales.

Let's walk through a real-life example of how A/B testing of your emails can help to improve your click-through rates, and ultimately your video sales.

Paul, of Paul's Personal Training, started using Gbox to sell his online fitness videos to help consumers around the world get into shape from the comfort of their own homes.

In order to increase his video views, Paul decided to let his existing email list of 2000 subscribers (made up of past and present personal training clients, contacts in the fitness industry, his family, and friends) know that he was offering these videos for sale on his Gbox channel. Paul uses AWeber to host his email lists.

But before Paul sent out an email and left the conversion

rates up to luck, he decided to first put some thought into what his desired outcome of the email campaign was, and what he could do to A/B test his messages in order to improve his campaign over time.

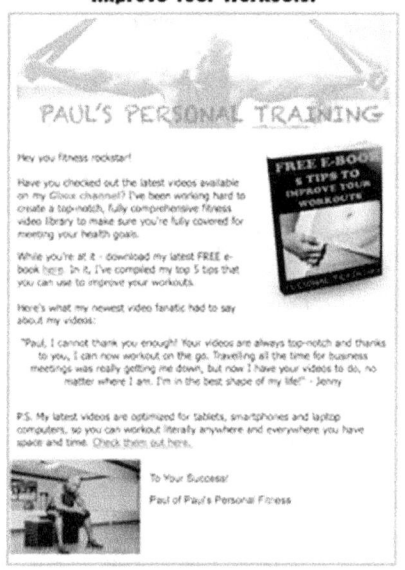

10% Open Rate = WINNER!

4% Open Rate

There are a number of things you can test in your email campaigns to find out what the magic formula for conversion is. Here are a few examples:

- Different subject lines.
- The use of video.
- The use of photos of yourself or your branding.
- Including social proof/testimonials.
- The size, color, text or placement of your "call to action" button.
- Including the price of your videos, or not, in the email body.
- The length of text in your emails.

- The inclusion of a "PS" at the end of your message with an additional call to action.
- The time of day you send your emails.
- Personalizing your emails by addressing them to the first name of the reader, or by beginning them generically.

Test Early - Test Often!

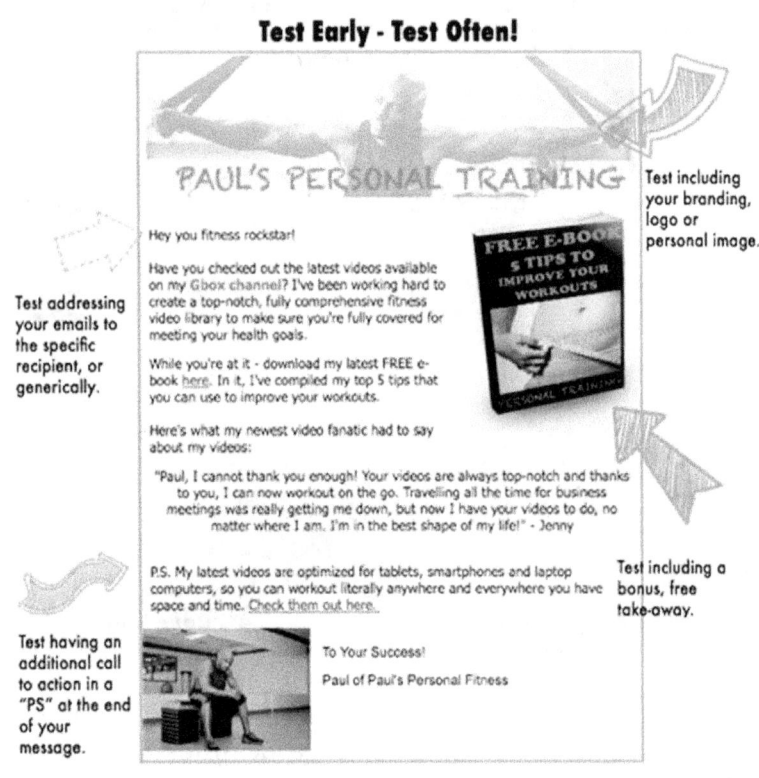

If you're looking to see higher open rates on your emails so that your list can get more information about you and build rapport, we recommend starting by testing different subject lines. If you're looking for higher click-through rates to your video channel, we recommend testing the use of videos and call to action buttons in your emails. These are just some of the many variations and examples of testing opportunities that exist.

For Paul, he wanted to double his click-through rate from

3% (which was his current average) to 6%. Determining this as his goal, the first A/B test he ran tested the use of video in his emails.

Best Practice: Although it may be tempting to test multiple things at once (ex: 2 different subject lines plus the use of video in your message), it is much more complicated to assess the results. We recommend testing only one variable at a time, and using the results to improve on your next message where you can then test something else.

Testing With Different Segments

When you run an A/B test of your email, you send one version of the message to one half of your email list, and a second version of the message to the other. Once you send out these messages and start seeing some of the stats, you can compare the results of the two emails to improve on the next one you send.

In Paul's case, he has 2000 subscribers on his email list, so he sent out version A of his email (WITH a video) to 1000 randomly selected subscribers, and version B of his email (withOUT a video) to the other 1000.

It's important to remember that when you're running these A/B tests, you send both versions at the same time (unless you're testing the time you send your emails of course!).

When is it not best practice to test all of your list at once?

If you already have a large email list, you can run smaller A/B tests with a quarter or a third of your entire list to first gauge the success of an email before sending the "winner" to the rest of the list.

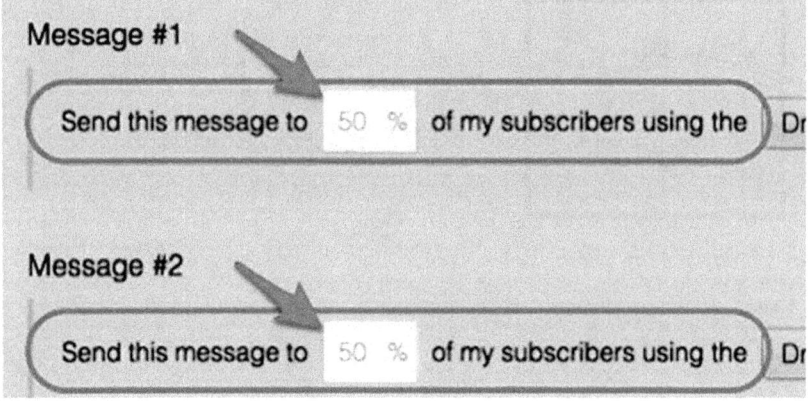

Another way to segment your email campaign is by keeping your existing and your prospective viewers on separate lists and targeting them using highly specific wording and marketing tactics.

For example, Paul sends his existing personal training clients more text-based emails that contain tips on how to enhance their workouts since he already has a rapport with them and sees most of them in person in their training sessions. To his list of potential consumers, he includes short videos of himself talking about his training methods and gives away free previews of his training videos to build trust and rapport.

Within these two groups he runs different A/B testing and tweaks each list's email formula based on their individual results.

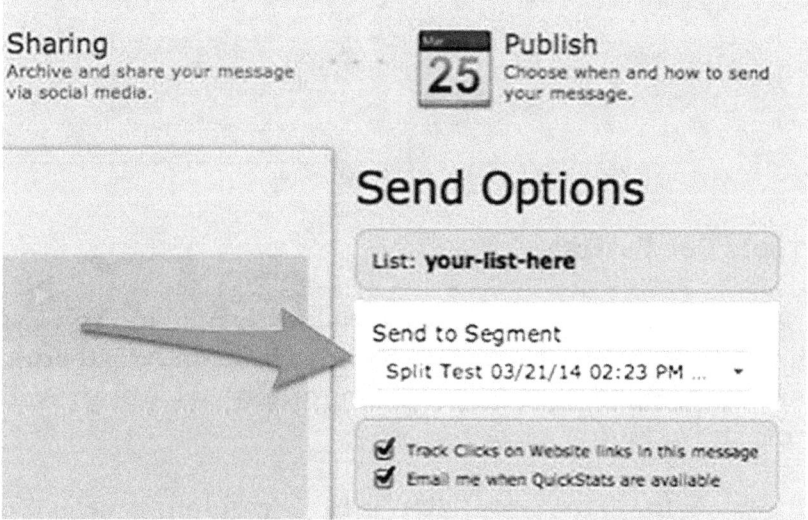

Best Practice: There are all sorts of ways to segment your email list to test out different emails (but do keep in mind that it's best to put these ideas into practice after you've already run a few A/B tests with your whole list and have determined what your highest converting emails look like).

Try separating your email list by gender or age; by people who have bought your videos before and those who haven't; people who have opened or clicked-through one of your emails in the past and those who haven't, etc.

**Test A of Call To Action Button
"Click Here"**　　　　**Test B of Call To Action Button
"Save 44%"**

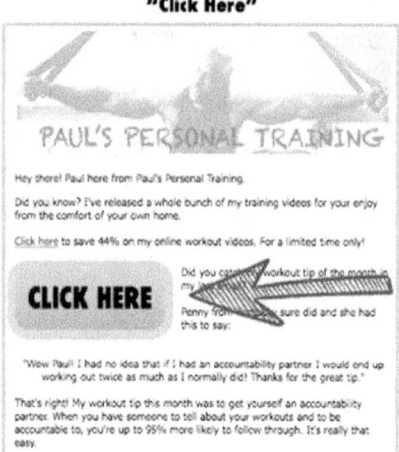

Tools For Testing

So how do you run a successful A/B test? If your specific email platform doesn't have built-in A/B testing systems, don't fret! You can manually set up an A/B test in just a few clicks.

First, split your email list into 2 randomly selected groups. Then, send one version of your email to the first group, and the second version to the second group. It's really that easy! The only extra step is having to compare the results yourself instead of having the results laid out for you. We recommend exporting your data to an excel spreadsheet to create a visual chart for easy comparison.

Don't have time to fuss with this extra step? AWeber[56], Mail Chimp[57], Campaign Monitor[58], HubSpot Email[59], Customer.io[60] and Active Campaign[61] are all email hosting services that have built-in A/B testing systems.

Best Practice: Remember, anything and everything about your emails can and should be tested. There are tons of tools out there (free and paid) designed specifically for you to test your email campaigns. There are a number of testing resources available[62] for you to compare and choose one that's right for your video business.

Create A Split Test

Split testing is an easy way to compare broadcasts against each other to see which performs better. More info

How many broadcasts would you like to include in this split test?

[2 messages ▾]

Tell us about each message in this test. Need help picking a subscriber percentage?

Message #1

Send this message to [50 %] of my subscribers using the [Drag & Drop Email Builder ▾]

Message #2

Send this message to [50 %] of my subscribers using the [Drag & Drop Email Builder ▾]

[Save Split Test]

Chapter 4: Analyze The Results Of The Campaign

So now that you have the results from your first A/B test, how do you determine the winner? First, think back to what your goal for this campaign was. How did you initially define what "success" meant for you in this campaign?

Now that you've seen what your audience responds to and have some numbers to work with, use these to create a larger email campaign.

Paul's original goal was to increase his click-through rate from 5 to 8%. He had seen with his previously sent emails that his click-through rate was hovering at the 5% mark, and he really wanted to see a significant increase of his list clicking through to viewing his Gbox video channel.

With the first test he ran comparing the use of videos in his emails, the email he sent out with a video in it got a click-through rate of almost 10%! The email without a video stayed at an average 6% so he had a clear winner.

Opens Over Time
Number of opens over the past 30 days for all lists.

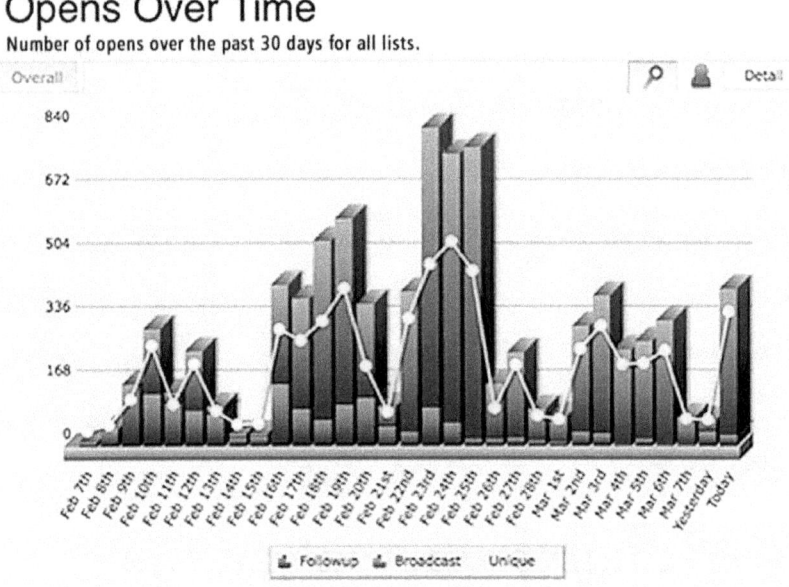

But he didn't stop there. The next email he tested compared the use of a call to action button and a video, versus just a video. From there he then tested different headlines, adding more images, adding more than one call to action, etc. Can you see how vast and endless the possibilities are?

Best Practice: Testing takes time and patience. After one A/B test you might see that using a video in your email is better than not using a video, but then the next time you send out a video-based message, your click-through rates are back to normal. This means that it could have just been the newness of your audience seeing a video in one of your emails for the first time that prompted them to click through. Keep testing different aspects of your emails to keep growing your email marketing campaign. Remember, every email you send is the opportunity to get some valuable feedback on what is going to make your audience convert.

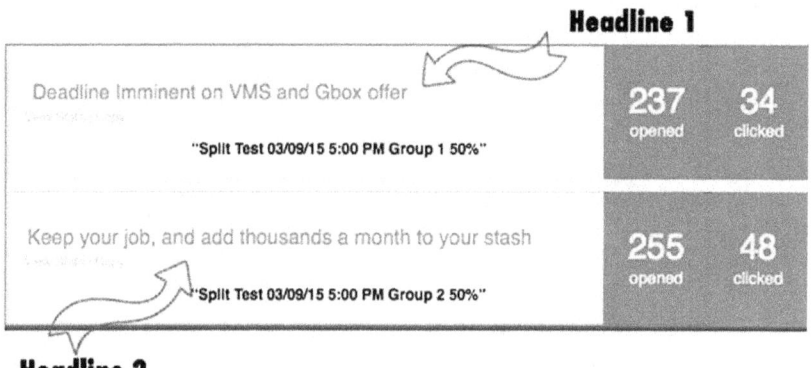

Headline 1

Headline 2

What Is A Successful Email Campaign?

Ultimately you want to increase your video sales and keep your consumers coming back for more. A successful email campaign has a high click-through rate to your video channel, but more importantly than that, your email list is actually converting to paying viewers.

Some things you don't want to see resulting from your email campaign are high unsubscribe rates (which means your list considers your messages as spam or irrelevant) or high bounce rates (meaning your email list is out of date).

Once you find the formula for the email format you send out that has the highest click-through rate, continue tweaking to focus on your conversions. This starts with creating awesome video content your audience loves, but can also include things such as running contests[63] [64], sending out surveys, and co-creating with your audience to highlight your online community.

Best Practice: Use A/B email testing to develop your email deliverability, your reputation and your overall rapport with your email list. Keeping track of your email campaign performance helps determine which direction to move in to increase your conversion rates and ultimately your bottom line. Using a service such as Webtrends[65], Abtasty[66] Click Throo[67], or Optimizely[68] to test your email campaigns helps to take the guesswork out of the analytics and data you collect.

TEST A:
WITHOUT Video

TEST B:
WITH Video

Hey, Sweta here from Gbox.

How is your video selling business doing? Have you been putting in some time and effort to evaluate your existing marketing systems? You will get the most out of the Live Marketing & Video Selling Webinar happening on Monday, February 23 at 12PM PSTIf you have already taken some time to think about your current marketing systems. We will be going through all sorts of social network tips, pricing formulas, profit maximizing strategies, and so much more!

Our in-house marketing guru, Sweta, has put together a video where she talks about her favorite Social Media Hack to give you a glimpse at some of the great information that you're going to be learning in our webinar. Click here to watch.

In case you missed it, here is another mini marketing video with some great tips to help get you excited for the Live Marketing & Video Selling Webinar.
· What It Takes To Get Videos Ranked on the Top Search Engines

Looking forward to meeting you soon!

Sincerely,
Sweta from Gbox
Gbox Support Team
support@gbox.com

Hey, Sweta here from Gbox.

Our in-house marketing guru, Sweta, has put together a video where she talks about her favorite Social Media Hack to give you a glimpse at some of the great information that you're going to be learning in our webinar. Click here to watch.

In case you missed it, here is another mini marketing video with some great tips to help get you excited for the Live Marketing & Video Selling Webinar.
· What It Takes To Get Videos Ranked on the Top Search Engines

Looking forward to meeting you soon!

Sincerely,
Sweta from Gbox
Gbox Support Team
support@gbox.com

How Often Should You Review Your Campaigns?

The best thing about setting up automated campaigns is that you can set them and forget them, right?

Not exactly. We recommend that at least once every three months you sit down and review all of your campaigns. This means, sit down and update all of your templates, the tone, and the branding for the campaign based on the results of your A/B testing and analytics.

If you are just starting it is most important to do this so you can stay congruent to your core audience and core messaging strategy.

We suggest you set a reminder message in your campaign early on to check, and give them a good scrubbing every three months.

Chapter 5: Your Ultimate Video Marketing Sales Funnel

Let's take a moment to run through a quick checklist to assess what you already have in place before walking through the ideal sales funnel for your video channel.

What is the message you want to be spreading through your video channel? Do you have a specific talent/passion? Want to raise money for a cause? Fund your start-up? Help people live better, or easier lives? No matter what the dream is for your video channel, you must be clear on your message in order to realize it.

Write down some of the current, specific goals you have for building your video channel. Are you trying to increase your social media reach? Add 500 new subscribers to your email list? Triple your video views? Become a featured

Gbox channel[69] with your success story?

Now think back to your target audience. Who is your core audience? Have you created an ideal client profile? Write down all the defining features of who your ideal viewers are: their wants and needs, buying behavior, interests and personality traits. The sales funnel you create is going to be aimed 100% at these people, so it's important to define exactly who they are.

Now that you've taken a good look at your video business model, ideal customer and desired outcomes, let's dive into the task of creating a sales funnel. This sales funnel process actually looks like a funnel, with your potential viewer at the top, and your desired outcome at the bottom.

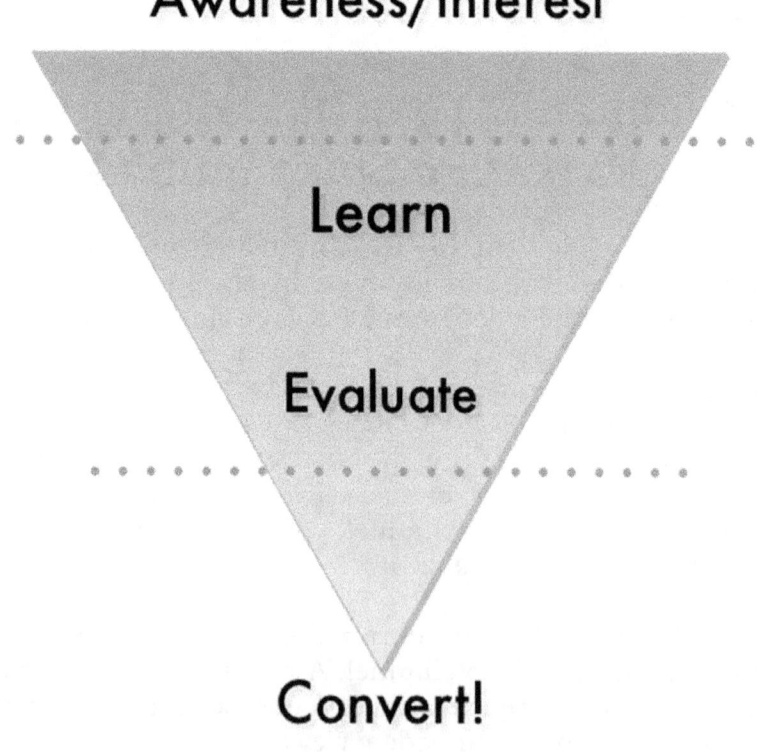

Awareness/Interest

Learn

Evaluate

Convert!

One of our featured Gbox channels, and total success stories, are the Super League rugby team, Hull FC[70] from Yorkshire England.

They have recently launched their Hull FC LIVE site powered by Gbox, and have been converting hundreds of new viewers thanks to the sales funnel we helped them implement.

Here is an example of what a video sales funnel looks like:

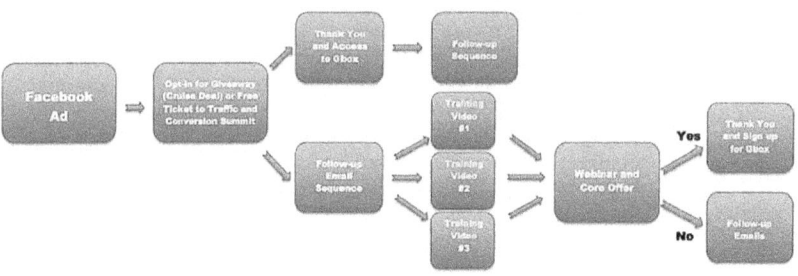

Remember to visit www.GboxVideoProfits.com to gain access to even more free marketing resources to help you implement your very own Video Sales Funnel.

Now follow along as we break down the steps you need to take, and show you some real-life examples of Hull FC's sales funnel and how it worked for them.

Awareness/Interest

Attract your audience's attention to create awareness of your videos.

Be authentic, creative and inspiring!

Chapter 6: Above The Funnel - Start With Lead Generation

To attract your viewers, you need to wave a big, brightly colored flag and shoot off fireworks to get their attention (metaphorically speaking of course!).

You need to pique their interest by offering them some super exciting content, and it needs to be enticing enough that they're convinced to give you a bit of information about themselves.

Here are some examples of high-interest topics you can leverage to initially attract your audience into your funnel:

Contests/Giveaways

What better way to attract potential viewers than to offer them something FREE they can win!? Contests are inherently awesome and attractive to anyone and everyone. Use videos to talk about the contest, show off what they can win, and tell them about how to enter. Check out our past posts on how to create the perfect viral video contest[71], and how to best launch and market it[72] for the step-by-step process of creating a successful contest (find the links to these articles in the "Tools and Resources" section at the back of this book). Capture their email address, or get them to follow you on social media in order for them to enter. Now they're in your funnel!

ENTER TO WIN!
A Signed HULL FC Jersey!

HULL F.C.

Name: Email:

Your Best Of The Best

Leverage the popularity of something you've already created. Compile a highlight reel, or re-package your number 1 video to include additional information from you - maybe an interview at the beginning where you talk about why you created the video and why it was so popular, or add a part to the end where you follow up with new information that makes it even more relevant. Leverage its existing popularity to attract a new set of viewers.

Hull FC puts together free, weekly "Plays Of The Week" videos. These highlight reels are short, action-packed and see huge viral sharing across social media platforms. Capturing their prospect's name and email address to view the video, their list grows weekly due to the popularity of these videos.

FREE VIDEO
Top 10 INSANE PLAYS
of the week!

Trust us, you do not
want to miss these!

Enter Your Name and
Email To View:

Name: Email:

HIGHLIGHTS: HULL **FC**

Top 10 INSANE PLAYS
of the week!

How-To's & Resources

People love to learn about how to make their lives better
and easier. Life-hacks, how-to's, the resources you love to
use - adding your personal spin to any of these topics is a
great way to help potential viewers get to know you better
and to see you as someone they value and trust. Leverage
a topic that's currently trending on social media and add
your own voice.

Whatever route you choose (and we suggest you create
content in each of these areas, and more) include Call To
Action pop-outs and buttons in your videos that direct the
viewer to your website or a landing page where you can
capture their information and move them onto the next
step of the funnel.

READ THIS FREE E-BOOK

**Paul's Personal
Training Presents...
"5 TIPS TO IMPROVE
YOUR WORKOUTS"**

FREE E-BOOK
5 TIPS TO
IMPROVE YOUR
WORKOUTS

PERSONAL TRAINING

Click Here For Free Instant Access »

Integrated with
Email Client

Free, informative E-Book
as "ethical bribe"
builds trust and rapport

Chapter 7: Middle Of The Funnel

This is where your potential consumer's crucial thought processes are happening. They've engaged with you and given you their information because they're attracted to what you have to offer them. Now you need to show them how their lives will be improved if they purchase one of your videos.

This is the evaluation phase. Your consumer is evaluating you, and you are evaluating your consumer.

In this middle portion of the funnel, you're also going to be determining whether or not the potential consumer is actually suited for what you're offering. Maybe you attracted someone into your funnel based on a giveaway you ran, but upon closer look, they aren't even close to your ideal client.

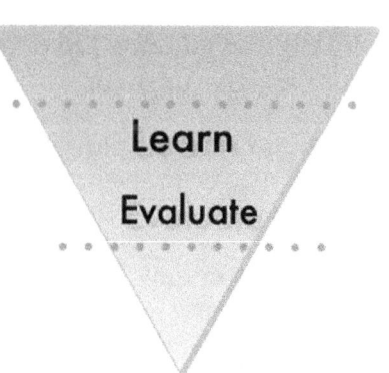

Teach your audience about your video channel and what you can offer them.

Evaluate leads to determine if they're a good match for your content.

Learn

Evaluate

In Hull FC's case, when they ran a contest to capture emails into their funnel, they got a ton of entries from sports fans in general, not necessarily rugby fans. This was a great learning opportunity, because many of these prospects were not interested in their videos, but only in the contest, and quickly opted out of their email list and social media pages after the contest closed.

But this should not be seen as a bad thing. Attracting life-long consumers only happens when you weed out the people who aren't helping to grow your video business. The contest did attract a lot of ideal rugby fans into the funnel, so it was still a success.

This is where you determine if your lead is a good fit for what you have to offer them.

Evaluate

If they are not your ideal customer, they will never convert!

At this point in the funnel, through your social media pages, email campaigns, and individual contact with consumers, you need to offer them some great content that really speaks to them.

This can come in many forms. Here are some ideas:

Interviews

Film an interview with a local celebrity, the executives at your company, or one of your dedicated viewers. These influencers have large social media followings themselves that you can also leverage. The more popular they are, the more weight their endorsement holds in the eyes of potential consumers.

Hull FC posts exclusive interviews with their star players, as well as insight from key rugby commentators immediately after each game the team plays. These videos are massively popular with their die-hard fans and get tons of shares which bring in new viewers. These new viewers submit

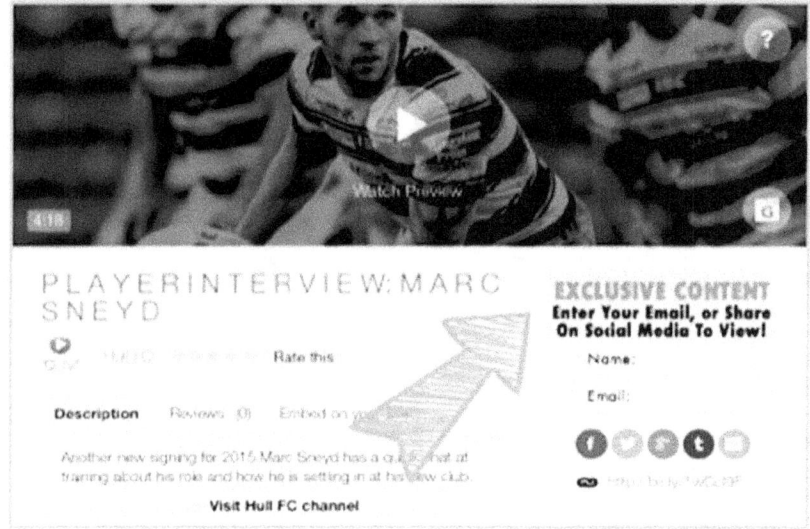

their email information to view the exclusive videos, and are entered into the sales funnel at this point.

Free Takeaways

Create a PDF, white paper, free report, video training series, or graphic to give away to your customers that helps them in their daily lives. At Gbox, we love creating free guides to help our creators improve their video sales. When you use your expert knowledge to create something informative and useful for your consumer, they will remember you every time they use it, and they will be prompted to pay for your content once they see that it actually works for them.

Hull FC leveraged this by creating free e-books containing transcribed interviews of their key players, never-before-released team photos, and player profiles. They saw over 500 new subscribers through opt-ins for their first free PDF alone!

Are you a die-hard **Hull FC** Fan? Check out this free, exclusive report containing never before seen interviews, player profiles and bonus material!

Enter your email to get it sent straight to your inbox!

Email:

Testimonials/Transformations

Do you have a sports or fitness channel? You're a makeup or hair whiz? DIY guru? Leverage your testimonials and transformations to educate viewers. Remember, this is the evaluation stage of the funnel - the more you're able to say "Look! Check out how my videos actually work to change people's lives!" the more they'll be convinced to purchase your videos.

 **box**

Hey there Gbox user,

Today I want to introduce you to someone really special.

Meet Parker. He began using Gbox just over a month ago on a whim. He had been sending out free tutorial videos to his software company's clients to help them through solutions to their software problems.

Because of their popularity with his clients, he saw Gbox as an interesting option for distributing these videos.

I'll let Parker tell you the rest...

Make it personal by adding a photo

"I cannot say enough good things about Gbox. First thing, of course, is the fact that I've added 15% to my business's monthly revenue by selling my videos. But more than that, I have been able to reach a way larger market than I even knew existed for my products. And it just keeps getting better! Thanks for making this such a hassle free way to turn my videos into profit." - Parker

To Your Video Empire Success
Sweta From Gbox
Follow Gbox on **Facebook** and **Twitter!**

Chapter 8: End Of The Funnel - Convert!

You've attracted potential consumers, captured their information, given them an epic taste of your content, and weeded out anyone who isn't your ideal consumer, so now it's time to convert. The people who are getting closer and closer to converting are waiting for you to give them the final push they need to purchase.

This part of the funnel is a critical part of your success and an on-going part of your overall marketing plan.

Your followers on social media, subscribers to your video channel, and the people on your email list should be engaged with often and regularly to be reminded of how awesome you are, and how they're missing out on something great if they don't buy your videos.

In addition, this portion of your funnel is also beneficial for those who have already purchased a video from you. It reminds them of how great your content is, tells them about new content you have to offer, and prompts them to be a repeat, lifelong viewer.

Nurture, nurture, nurture!

Create loyal, life-long fans with consistent, quality content.

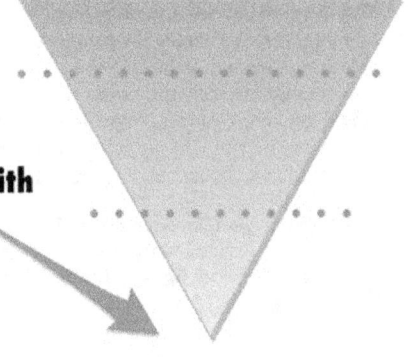

Convert!

Video Nurture Campaign

Create email newsletters that are video-centric. Videos are known to improve click-through rates in emails, plus they build trust and rapport with your audience by exposing them to you and your brand. Include things like a tip of the day, spotlight on one of your audience members, invitation to an online event or webinar, or a personal story. Anything that is informative and valuable to your audience works well here.

Personal Check-In

Email or direct message your followers to see if there's anything they need. Personally email them in order to introduce yourself and ask them what problems they have in their life to see how you can help. Then link them to videos you have already created to answer their questions, or create a new video just for them. Individual attention and authentic human connection goes a long way in converting consumers.

Surveys

You can't keep selling without understanding your consumer base inside and out. Create incentivizing surveys so they feel involved in the content creation process. Follow the rule of commerce, which focuses on creating content that consumers want so they can bring you back value in return. This value may be referring your videos to others. We try to focus on creating two surveys a month to receive consumer feedback. In return we give away branded SWAG, which incentivizes the audience to participate.

You can also use their information to tailor content to them, or direct them to content you've already created that you think they will benefit from. This is a great way to come up with new content to engage even more viewers, and get some valuable feedback on your existing content. We like using Typeform[73] and Qualaroo[74] to create our surveys.

Hey Hull FC Follower!
We want to know more about you
CLICK HERE
to fill out a 1-minute survey
And we'll send you a free gift!

HULL F.C.
Est. 1865

Discounts

Membership sure does have its privileges, and your list wants to hear about how special they are just for being a subscriber. Plus, who doesn't love a good discount? Offer your subscribers flash sales and discounts on your videos in order to help convince those on the verge of converting. The next section of this book goes into detail about how to use pricing strategies such as discounts to increase your sales and profits.

Chapter 9: Additional Resources

Here are a few additional resources for you to use when creating your email marketing campaigns and video sales funnel.

Ad Remarketing

Use Facebook remarketing and display ads to drive traffic to your designated landing pages. You can set this up through Adroll[75] and Facebook Remarketing to target the people that went to your landing pages but didn't subscribe. Now you can take them to a landing page that really sells your blog, newsletter, or other videos.

HelloBar

This is the best tool to drive "zombie" traffic to a subscribe page. For example, if your home page is not receiving much traffic then you can add a HelloBar[76] that links to your most popular page or item on your site that is receiving traffic.

What Page Really Sells Your Offer?

When you create a blog post or an email, send them to a social network or landing page that really sells your videos and what you do. For example, send them to a landing page and ask them to subscribe to your other offers.

HULL F.C.

Hey there Hull FC SuperFan!

We played the York City Knights last night and boy, was it a great game.

We know you're a super fan so of course you didn't miss it!

Include a large Call To Action so they don't miss it!

But, did you know that our captain, Gareth Ellis, gave an exclusive interview after the game?

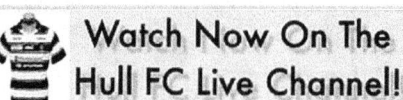

Watch Now On The Hull FC Live Channel!

You can also catch all our latest videos including match re-caps and the latest analysis from the coaches.

We can't wait for you to see all the exclusive content.

James Ray
Hull FC Fan Club Manager

Responsive Design

In order to make your landing page responsive for mobile phones and across devices, you must take 3 simple steps.

• Download a responsive theme for your landing page from Themeforest[77].

• Use an email template from GitHub[78] that is mobile friendly.

• Then use Litmus[79] to test everything to ensure it is mobile friendly. More and more people are using mobile devices to check their emails. You don't want to miss out on their business.

There are many great resources online that go over responsive design in terms of email marketing.

How Do You Ensure The Email Reaches The Inbox?

Just because you send emails doesn't necessarily mean they will reach your subscriber's inbox. Here is why they may not be reaching the inbox:

- Content is everything. Despite what anyone tells you about email deliverability, the content will determine whether it ends up in SPAM or not.

- Another reason may be the complaint rate. If this is high (meaning more than 10 complaints) then your email reputation will suffer and it will reduce the chance of the emails reaching the inbox.

- Now say that you send 10,000 emails today and 0 emails tomorrow. This will impact your deliverability rate and how the emails reach the end user.

- Make sure you have the correct DNS records set up to ensure success when it comes to deliverability.

Start by looking at some data on Mail Tester[81] and Sender Score[82].

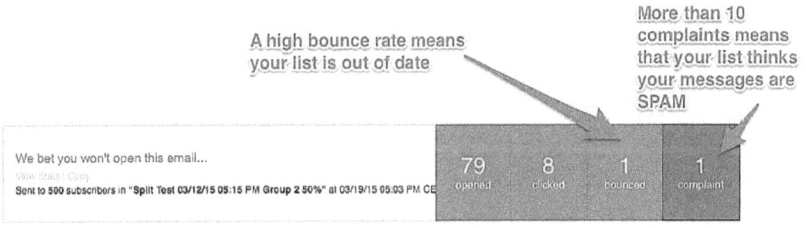

What You Need To Know About Images

60% of your subscribers have images blocked in the emails they receive. What can you do to get around this?

This is when you can get creative with your messaging, and design around this. Who said you need images to make it look good? Just use an incredible template.

We recommend visiting Campaign Monitor[83], Themeforest[84] or Templateria[85] for email templates.

Image Alt Tags

Don't forget to use ALT tags in your images. If it is an HTML image then you can add an "alt" attribute to it.

What is the text you want the image to reveal in the case that it doesn't show up? This should be keyword rich.

HTML Text Is The Way

It is pointless to send an email if it is not going to be seen by your target audience. This is why you should consider using plain HTML text in your emails instead of using a huge image with the words inside the image.

This section of the book is the largest for a reason. Email marketing is one of your key tools for converting consumers, which is why it's so important to do correctly.

Use your emails to educate, engage and inspire your consumers. This is the key to conversions.

In the next Chapter we take you through some of our top pricing strategies that actually work, how to build a story around your content, the value of co-creation and how to simplify the whole process.

SECTION 4

The Perfect Pricing Model For Your Videos

The good news is that there aren't any fixed rules about pricing strategies. But the bad news is that if you price your content wrong, you risk missing out on profits. At the end of the day you want to get as many views as possible, at the maximum price possible. So where do you start?

Bottom Line: The price of a video can be the differentiator between something that sells and something that doesn't. Pricing your videos involves learning more about your target audience and how much they really value what you do. If they do not value you or your content at all, then they will expect you to give it to them for free, or they will purchase it somewhere else they find has more value.

Think of pricing not as the cost, but as the perceived value of your video content by your specific customer. Too often content owners determine their pricing through the hours and cost it took to create it. This will result in zero sales for your video business.

How happy are your consumers to buy something from you? That is the big indicator of price.

This portion of the book was created as one of the final aspects of your video selling profit stream creation. We want to help you develop your pricing strategy so you can deliver more to your consumers.

We created this pricing strategy section to help those who are struggling with pricing their videos.

The Gbox team created Gbox because we wanted to take a stand when it comes to pricing valuable content. Why? We strongly believe that our content creators should be paid what their content is worth. Many other networks cannot attest to that. We make it feasible for our content creators to determine the correct pricing for their audience and then easily implement pricing around their audience's preferences. Why stick with a fixed price, when you can create a pricing strategy that matches your audience's desires?

We always get asked about how to effectively price videos for an audience.

This portion of the book will teach you:

• What you need to know in terms of pricing strategies

• The impact of your pricing on sales, and

• How to test the pricing strategy you go with.

We want to help you create value for your audience.

So let's start here: Your audience determines your pricing strategy. But sometimes it's difficult to read the minds of your target audience.

Chapter 1: Why Does Pricing Matter?

Pricing sets the experience for your audience. The price determines how much they value you and the content you're putting out there. Everyone has a different preference and opinion, so don't take it personally if they are expecting to view your content for free.

Sometimes it is important for you to allow your audience to "sample" your videos before selling them any content on your website.

You can create "sample" trailers that you upload to YouTube with a link to your Gbox channel for the premium version of your content.

You can educate your audience using webinars and then have them purchase through your Gbox channel. This is the exact strategy Video Marketing Scholars[86] carried out with a series of informative webinars.

You can use a survey email sequence and find out how much your audience is willing to pay for your content. Ask them: "from $0 to $100,000, what are you willing to pay for this video?" This will infuse a sense of humor into the conversation and prompt answers from you target audience that you can use to price your videos.

Chapter 2: How To Increase Your Perceived Value

When you increase the perceived value of your content, you will always get more money. Increasing your perceived value gives you more room to move the price point up. How do you get people to feel your value is higher? Perceived value is the gap between the price, and how much value your customers believe it delivers.

Marketing increases perceived value. For example, say that you own a huge video collection and your consumers want to share your videos with their personal audience. If you charge 25 cents for all the marketing materials (graphics, custom landing pages, email templates, etc.) that come with your collection, then you have just increased the perceived value of your videos.

The other way to increase your perceived value is by providing big solutions for big problems. When you identify a pain point your market has and offer them a guaranteed solution, you can charge significantly more for your solution than someone who cannot guarantee the solution.

Oftentimes, we create our pricing based on how much the

cost of labor is to produce the final masterpiece. This is not best practice for creating your pricing structure, because creators generally spend significantly more hours creating something than it takes for the audience to consume it. When a feature film is created, it can cost millions of dollars. The pricing structure for films is based on getting a high frequency of views (at a reasonable price per view) because of the high perceived value of the film.

The greatest perceived value of a video is when it is new and first released. When your audience loses interest, the value goes down. You always want to charge at the point of the highest perceived value.

Then there are businesses where the perceived value stays constant over time. These businesses can use a subscription based payment structure and regularly release new, relevant content for their viewers to ensure continued customer loyalty.

Then there are models where the perceived value increases over time. This can be carried out using Gbox's "Name Your Price" model, where the audience has the power to determine the price they want to pay. The more your audience gets to know and trust your content, the more they are willing to pay over time.

When the perceived value is in the future, you want to build the emotional connection to your video before you charge your audience.

This is based on the ideology of how you can keep them coming back time after time. This is more of a freemium model ("free to play" like gaming, Zynga; or "like freemium" such as Evernote, Dropbox and so forth). In Gbox this is known as the "Fundraising" model where you can allow your consumers to contribute to your video the amount they wish, after they view it.

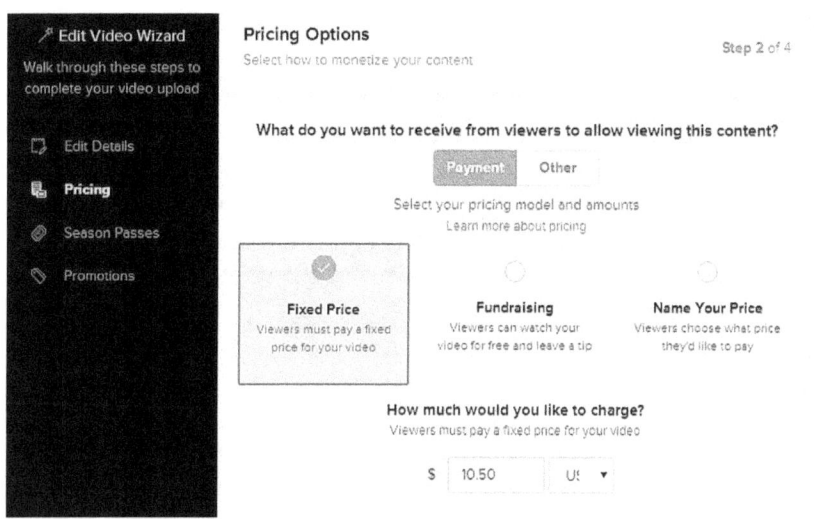

Chapter 3: Value, Quality & Community

The first thing that needs to be mentioned before deciding on a pricing strategy is the fact that people are always willing to pay for quality content. They're even willing to pay a lot for it, so long as the value of that content is high and brings something tangibly positive and beneficial to their lives. When you're new to the video selling business and it comes to pricing strategies, the actual price of what you charge your audience is somewhat of a guessing game until you are more established and have experimented with different amounts and strategies. The bottom line is: consistently create quality content and you will build a large following of devoted viewers who will pay whatever you ask for your videos because they know the value of your content is worth the price tag.

The second point we think is important to make before delving into pricing strategies, is that building a large, devoted fan base is more profitable in the long run than making money right away off of high priced videos.

129

Oftentimes creators get discouraged when they aren't immediately seeing the views they thought they would, or they have to charge a lot less than they believe their content is worth in order to get views. If you are able to grow a substantial audience and you consistently release quality content for them, over time they will start paying for your videos. It just takes time, dedication and authentic connection building. Focus on building your community and the revenue will come!

Know Your Competition

The best place to start is by researching your competitors and seeing how much they are charging for their videos. This is also a great tip that relates to marketing tactics and your video channel growth in general - knowing who your competitors are, tracking their views, and analyzing the marketing tactics they use helps you to see where you can either do better, or areas you can push into that aren't already being explored in your niche market.

Look at what your competitors are charging for their videos to get an idea of the price range you can be charging in. Of course, if you think your content is worth more, you can charge more, but it's good to have a general idea of what your niche market is already used to paying.

Know Your Market

The next bit of research you should do is reach out to your existing audience and ask them what they're willing to pay for your content. Direct message some of your followers on Twitter, Instagram, Facebook, or whatever social media pages you use, and ask for their opinion. Send out personalized messages to your email list giving them a new video to watch, and in return ask them to give you feedback on how much they would have been willing to pay for the video. Run a contest on your social media pages getting your followers to fill out a survey about the value and pricing of your content, and offer a randomly selected winner branded swag.

Again, this is a great tip that applies to all facets of your video channel development, as well as to determining your best pricing strategy. Create a 3-5 question survey for your followers asking them about how much they value your content, what they are willing to pay for your content, what they would like to see more or less of on your channel, and any other feedback they have for you. Asking your audience directly, and then really listening to their feedback is the best way to grow your business.

It's important to remember that how you think you're perceived by your audience, how you want to be perceived by your audience, and how you're actually perceived by your audience, can be hugely different. The only way to find out how to grow your audience and keep delivering content that they find valuable and are willing to pay for, is by asking them and then adjusting accordingly to their wants and needs.

What Are The "Hot Buttons?"; Customer Segmentation And Why It Matters

We all have "hot buttons" or emotional triggers. People hardly ever make a purchase through pure logic. Most of the time their decisions are emotionally driven. No two people will perceive your video content the same way. When you are able to understand these different groups you will be able to identify the "hot buttons" that cause them to buy from you. How are your consumers interacting with your video content? Are they engaged? Do they feel as though the content is relatable to them? Different groups of people should have different options. This means you will have to create laser specific content to meet your consumer needs.

131

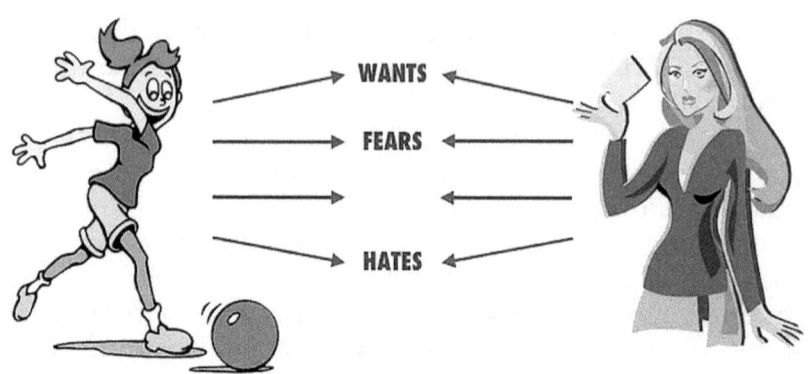

WANTS

FEARS

HATES

Once you segment these different groups, then you will be able to create pricing for each of these different groups. You will want to separate each of these groups in your email platform. They should each be in a separate list. This way when you send out video updates, each group receives the video priced specifically to them.

Best Practice: create a separate tone and voice to match each group. The more you can resonate with your audience the more they will purchase from you.

If you can describe the consumer's problem better than they can, and then over-deliver on the solution, then they will become a loyal buyer.

How To Brand A Product To Increase Its Value

The first way to brand yourself to increase your perceived value is to refer to the ideal customer profile you created earlier. This ideal customer profile will help you determine the price your audience wants to pay for your content.

Your brand can tell someone that you cater to sophisticated people with lots of disposable income, or you can brand yourself in a way that attracts easy going, middle-class people. The image you create around your videos and the community you build depends on your content.

Let's walk through a real life example: Paul's Personal Training Studio.

Paul charges anywhere from $50-150/hour for his personal training sessions. However, he engages with his online community by using Gbox to sell his personal training videos and courses online. He brands himself to serve a market of people who aren't exactly the 100% committed health addicts who can afford personal training sessions with him, but they are trying to become more healthy by purchasing online fitness videos. His market is in the mid-average range in terms of income. Paul brands himself to be the "motivator" for this particular market. This means he doesn't dress in business suits, nor does he charge a ton of money for his services.

Paul packages his training videos in a way that speaks to his target audience. He dresses in sports clothing and comes across as an active and educated health expert.

Paul's "Hot Button": His customers can use his services and watch his videos to live a vivacious lifestyle, or they can feel fatigued and overweight all the time.

Branding affects the way you price. What does your brand say about you?

Chapter 4: Pricing Strategies

Decoy Pricing Model

In order to set a price, you need to first create a hypothesis that you can A/B test to determine the best pricing strategy for your business. Having a starting point and then using other analytics to refine it is the best way to come up with the "magic number" that works for your business. Pricing is based on judgment (which is often arbitrary), it is not based on math.

For example, say that you offer three different types of pricing. One is a one-time video cost of $3.99; a season pass for $27.00 that lasts a year; or the combination which gives your customers access to all the NEW $3.99 videos you create plus all the videos in the $27.00 season pass, and this combination pass also sells for $27.00. Which one would most people opt for?

| $3.99 | $27.00 | $27.00 |
| Individual Video | Season Pass | Combo Pass |

We saw that most people bought the $27.00 combination pass and almost zero people bought the $27.00 season pass.

As the second part of our testing, we decided to leave off the $27.00 season pass. As a result we saw that most people purchased individual $3.99 videos. Why do you think this happened?

$3.99
Individual Video   $27.00
Combo Pass

This is known as the "decoy" pricing model where more expensive packages look more attractive next to a clearly inferior choice. People use this technique to make expensive items look affordable.

We found that the $27.00 season pass doesn't have a lot

of value as a package for our consumers, but has a huge influence over the way consumers make decisions.

When using this model it is important to go after greenfield customers. This means do not try to sell your content to your competitors' customers.

People tend to overvalue the things they already own/pay for, and it is more difficult to get someone to switch to something new than to find a new consumer.

Even if your content is 500 times better than your competitors', people tend to stick with what they already know and are paying for.

Two Types Of Pricing

There are two prices in the world: there are prices that are expensive and there are prices that are affordable. Expensive items require a substantial trade-off, and most likely involve a substantial thought process before making the decision. For example, "should I cancel my vacation this year so I can buy this MacBook Pro?"

When something is affordable, it doesn't require you to think twice about it. You just go for the purchase. In the end it is all about the value you deliver to the customer and how they find your content changing their current mood or solving a problem in their life.

Offering two different price levels can work for your videos. The first thing you may want to determine is which one is ideal for your customers and how they think. If your market normally shops at thrift or secondhand stores, then haut-couture pricing may not suit them.

Your branding and core messaging play a huge role when it comes to who you're attracting to your video content.

The Pricing Trilogy

The fair pricing model focuses on the consumption of your video content. You will be able to determine the pricing for each individual consumer based on how much content they consume. The more content they consume, the less they will have to pay to consume it. This is where the season pass pricing option built right into Gbox is most useful.

The more time your viewers opt-in for, the cheaper the pass is for them. Having multiple season pass options gives consumers more incentive to buy.

For example, viewers can opt to view any of your videos for one-month for $25.99. Or, they can get a six-month pass for $59.99, or a one-year pass for $99.99! Obviously the most economical deal is the year pass, and all it takes is a click of a button for you to create this deal.

Low-Pricing Options & Up-Sells

Some consumers want to purchase only when there is a low barrier to entry. You should charge them a very small price to watch the first few videos. Once you have won them over with your video collection, then upsell them other products or services you may offer. If you have other premium content, you can also offer them something more than they are already used to. The most important item here is to be as compelling as possible.

The downside of using this pricing strategy is that you may receive a lot of unqualified consumers because there is a low barrier to entry. However, the upside is that you will receive massive exposure to your brand because many people will engage with it. It all depends on the market you are trying to go after. What do your consumers expect from you?

High-Pricing Options & Funding A Marketing Campaign

Have you ever heard of Tesla's pricing model? Elon Musk's Tesla strategy was to create a high priced product for early adopters and use the profits to create something affordable for the masses. You can take this same strategy and implement it for your video pricing method.

Eventually you will want to build up a list of consumers who love your videos. In order to do this you may want to start off with a high barrier to entry. This will weed out all the unqualified prospects and keep only highly qualified prospects.

The downside of this strategy is that you may not receive as many prospects. You may only receive a few consumers at a time. The exposure will start off small, but the focus here is building long-term, devoted customers who will always come back for more of your content.

The upside of this strategy is that your list will be laser-focused and highly engaged. You will not have anyone on your list that is just sitting around and not contributing.

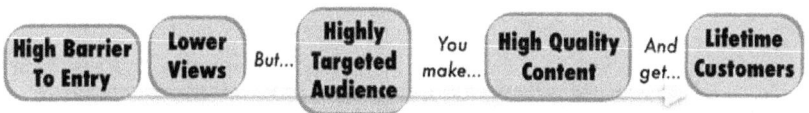

Design Pricing Models Based On Instant Judgments

People tend to make judgments about everything. In fact, most of the time people make decisions within a split-second before the brain can even apply any sort of logic or reasoning. For example, take a pair of UGGS. Even though the pricing on these shoes is fixed, people tend to make value judgments based on the positioning of the product. If a teenage girl wore UGGS in a picture, the consumer would believe it would cost a lot less than a businesswoman who wore UGGS with a sophisticated briefcase.

Instead of determining the value of the shoes and pricing it out, the consumer immediately asks, "how much would a sophisticated businesswoman pay for these shoes? How much would a high school student pay for these shoes?"

This is why positioning can help you determine the price for your content.

Chapter 5: Dollars & Cents

So you've done your research and now you have a better idea of what your competition is charging and roughly how much your audience says they're willing to pay for your videos. Now it's time to come up with a number.

In our research and extensive testing of different pricing strategies, we've discovered that it's best to come up with at least two prices for videos: a high price, and a low price. This speaks to the majority of your audience: people who are willing to pay for content, and people who aren't willing to pay much, or anything at all, for content. This can be addressed in a number of creative ways.

When you price your content with two different prices, and shape the difference around a limited quantity, or time-limited deal, this motivates your audience to buy. Coming up with an initial release price for early viewers (ex: "first 100 customers can view at $1.99! Regular price: $5.99) or putting a time limit on a price (ex: view for $1.99 for the next 24 hours! $5.99 after), is a great way to get views.

Another strategy is to offer two different versions of the same video: a regular version that you price at a low amount, and a "deluxe" edition that has extra footage, or some sort of added bonus, and is priced higher. On the one hand, you create a lower priced, easily accessible video that lots and lots of people are motivated to buy because of the high value of the content and the low price. This translates to higher views, but lower revenue.

On the other hand, you create added value with a deluxe edition of your videos that you might get less views on, but the revenue on each view is higher.

And, if you go above and beyond to impress your viewers and give them high value content in your deluxe edition videos, you will be fostering a long-lasting, trusting relationship with them that will ensure their continued devotion to paying for your videos.

$1.99
Regular Video

$5.99
Deluxe Version

The third way to make this multi-pronged pricing structure work for you is by going with a "Name Your Price" strategy. Gbox has this option built right into the platform.

When you upload a video, you can list the minimum price for viewers to pay, and then give a suggested price to help guide their decision.

This is also a great way to get feedback on your audience's perceived value of your content. Once you start seeing the prices they're willing to pay, you can adjust the prices of your videos moving forward to maximize your profitability.

Best Practice: Always give viewers two or more pricing options. This maximizes your sales by catering to a wide variety of viewers with different budgets and spending habits. Remember, you can change the pricing of your videos at any time, with a click of a button, using the Gbox platform.

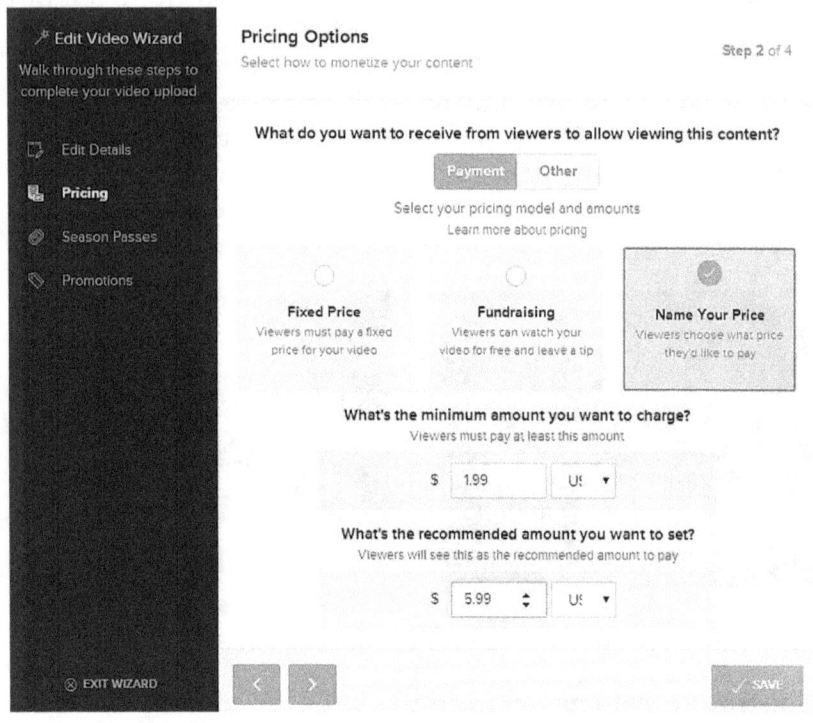

Paul's Personal Training

A great example to highlight these different pricing strategies in action is Paul's Personal Training business. Follow along as we walk you through this real life example of a Gbox user and how he uses Gbox to maximize his profitability by implementing multiple pricing strategies.

Paul started creating personal training videos that he sent to his existing personal training clients for them to use at home. These videos became so popular that he decided to use Gbox to see if he could make some money on the side in order to expand his business. Since he'd never done anything like this before, he was unsure about how to price these videos.

Luckily for Paul, Gbox has some great built-in pricing options that make it easy to test out different pricing strategies.

The first pricing strategy he used was "Name Your Price." He did this for two reasons; firstly, because he simply didn't know what to price his videos at, and secondly, because he wanted to give early adopters of his fitness videos the opportunity to experience the quality of his videos, without feeling discouraged by a price they weren't willing to pay.

He uploaded a number of his videos to his Gbox account, chose the "Name Your Price" option with a low minimum suggested amount, and then embedded the videos on his website and social media pages. In just over two months, Paul's videos had each gotten just over a hundred views, and he was able to get an idea of the price range his audience was willing to pay.

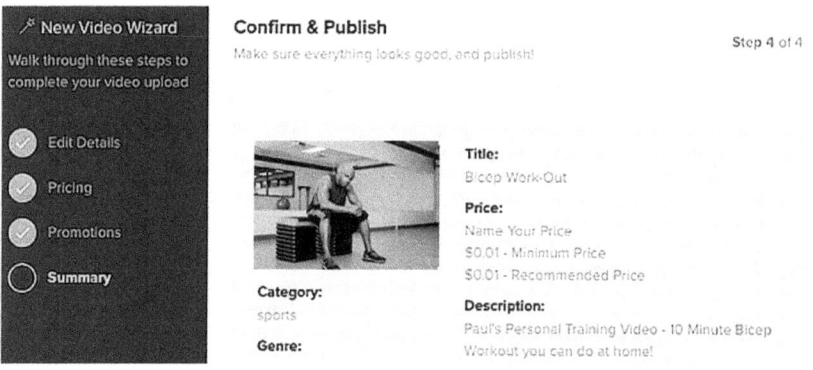

The second pricing strategy Paul used was the "Fixed Price" option. He uploaded his training videos to Gbox, priced them all at $9.99, which he found to be on the higher end of industry standard after doing some extensive research of both his competitors and niche market members, and analyzing the prices that viewers were choosing to pay through the "Name Your Price" option. He imbedded these videos onto his website for anyone to buy.

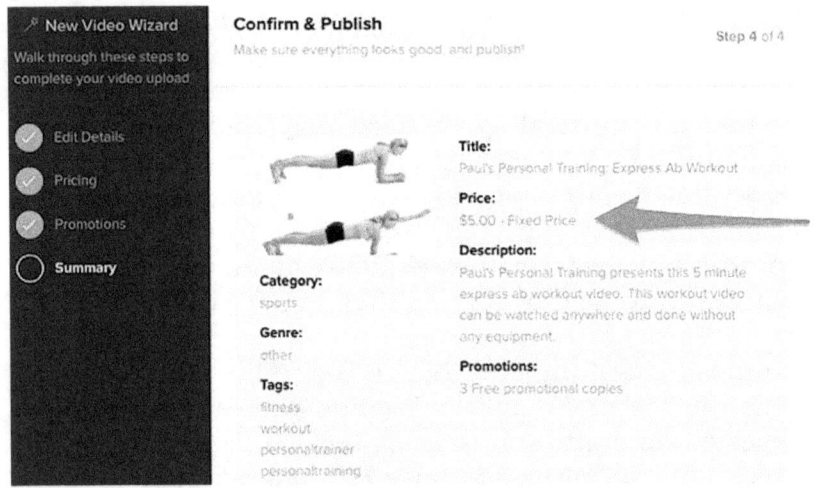

To cater to the portion of his audience that wasn't willing to pay that high of a price, he also offered discounts on his videos.

He advertised the same videos at the discounted price of $4.99, but had a time limit on them. To do this, he copied the video with one click on his Gbox channel, changed the price to $4.99, and then embedded these videos on a different part of his website that was only accessible through the links he posted on his social media pages and in his email newsletter.

He made this discount available for a limited time, and then took down the videos after the time was over.

The third pricing option built into the Gbox Platform is the fundraising option. This is a great way to interact with your audience and build trust and a lasting rapport with them.

Paul decided to create a limited edition personal training video that highlighted the issue of heart disease and the importance of maintaining regular physical activity.

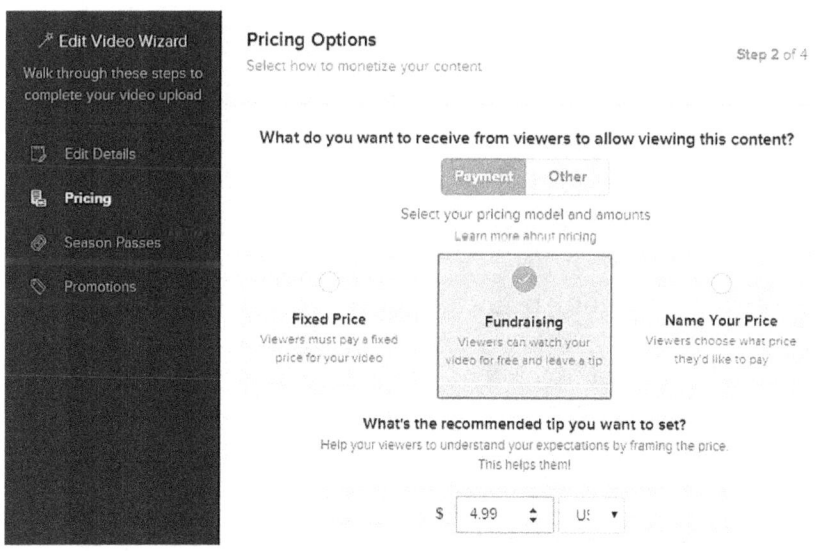

The "Fundraising" pricing option lets viewers make a donation of whatever amount they choose, after watching a video. Paul committed 75% of the money raised through this video to the Heart and Stroke Foundation.

This created awareness around a very important cause, built

rapport with his audience by giving them the opportunity to watch his videos to get to know him and the quality and benefits he brings to their lives, and motivated them to purchase his videos with the added benefit of knowing their money was going to a good cause.

The fundraising option is also great for crowdfunding a new venture your business has. Create a promotional video and ask viewers to donate towards a new event, product or any other sort of endeavor you want to fundraise for.

Focus on your audience's wants and needs, over-deliver quality content, adjust your pricing once you start seeing what they're willing to pay, and then watch your profits soar!

Remember, you can always adjust the price of your videos. Gbox makes it easy and instant to change the price of any of your videos. Don't get stressed out or caught up in the theory and multitude of pricing options. Start by putting a price on your video and see what happens!

Chapter 6: Storytelling Through Pricing

Stories about your brand and the content you sell make a huge difference when it comes to making more sales with your video content. Have you ever wondered why people are able to charge so much for something you know to have low value? They create a story behind it and around it to drive their sales.

How To Build A Story

Price serves as a proxy for quality. The price you set for your content influences the perceived value of your content. For example, most people are used to paying $50 for a bottle of wine in a nice restaurant, versus $10. They usually believe the $50 wine bottle is better than the $10 bottle of wine. This is because our society has been conditioned to pay a certain price for wine in nice restaurants, and if the price of a bottle of wine is lower than the "norm," our minds jump to the conclusion that there must be something lacking in the quality.

If you want to take the premium pricing route then you must have premium content to go with it. The best way to create premium content is by creating different versions of the content and charging the same price. This will help you determine which content resonates best with your target audience. The other way around this would be to create several different pricing options for the same video, This will help you determine what your target audience is willing to pay.

Your feature video should be created by reverse engineering from what your audience will feel like after they purchase a video from you. This is the process your audience should be set up to walk through. Remember, the outcome of your content will help you determine if they purchase from you again or not. Your content must leave them with a happy feeling, or solve a daily problem they are facing, because this sets the perceived value for your content.

Co-Creation & Adding Value

A great way to create content is by involving your target audience. This is the easiest way to build a marketing army around the content you create. This will not only help you distribute and promote your content, but you will actually be delivering what your customers want to be paying for.

No matter how much research we do, when it comes to creating new content we can never determine at 100% accuracy what our customers want. By allowing your consumers to help you develop your content, you are able to receive real-time feedback on their needs and wants.

This feedback will also help you determine pricing for your video content.

For example, create a video series with your target audience and actually include them (their picture, or a video clip) in the videos. If you do not want to include them, then you may want to add a piece about what they do and how they have contributed to your online community.

By adding this piece, you are able to not only build rapport for your brand but you are simultaneously building a marketing army for your branded video collection.

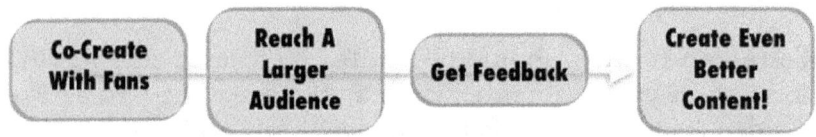

Chapter 7: How To Simplify The Process

The more options your target audience has, the longer they will take to make a decision. The longer it takes them to make a decision reduces the chances of a video sale being made.

The pricing placement also has an effect on how many sales are made. Sometimes it is better that the pricing shows up after the video has been shown to prevent the consumer from making a judgment before watching the preview of what you have to offer.

The more simplified the process is, the longer your consumers will stick around.

Flexibility Pricing Matters

Have you ever experienced a time where you worked really hard to achieve something and it didn't go your way? Then, something that was an "accident" happened to be a success? This is why your pricing structure needs to be flexible. Gbox provides this flexibility with their pricing models. Have you uploaded a video yet and started selling? Give it a shot!

Your pricing should change based on what your consumer experiences with your videos.

We suggest you start off by setting the price as "Name Your Price" to determine where your customer's head is at when it comes to the pricing of your videos.

Then once you understand the price point they are purchasing at, create more of the same content at that simple price.

You will start seeing your videos move as fast as hotcakes!

Customers Should Determine The Price For You

Let's perform a little exercise here. What goes through the mind of your consumer when they first interact with videos?

Make a list of all the items that may go through your consumer's mind as they approach your video. Are they thinking the price may be too high? What are they thinking about the positioning? If you can understand the consumer better than they understand themselves, you will succeed in the video business.

Eventually logic will kick in after a few purchases of your

videos. Will you be prepared for this? How can you be prepared to take charge as logic kicks in? For example, if your video is priced lower than industry norm, people will start wondering why it is priced so low. If you are offering free copies of your video to the world, people may begin thinking they are "cheap" and that is how they will brand you.

If your goal is to capture high spending customers with your messaging, they will analyze your videos no matter what. The higher the price is, the more thinking is involved. This could potentially ruin the chances of you getting exposure for your videos.

Personas Help Determine Price

Now you are beginning to understand pricing better for your current customer base. After you know which price point people are purchasing from then you can go ahead and create ideal customer profiles from them.

These profiles need to include:

- Consumer interests (What do they like to do in their free time?)

- Consumer purchasing behaviors (Do they purchase from the Internet? Stores?)

- Consumer basic information (age, sex, location)

- Consumer goals (What do they want to achieve in the near future?)

- Consumer frustrations (What makes them upset?)

- Consumer secret desires (What do they secretly desire? What keeps them up at night?)

- What makes them happy? (What do they like to do?)

- How would you describe your consumer's personality? (What does it feel like to hangout with them?)

After you answer all the questions above, draw out a persona that best fits your target audience and their preferences. Find out what they enjoy doing most and how they go about their daily activities.

How To Predict Pricing

Wouldn't it be awesome if we could get the pricing right every single time? Imagine if every time you exposed consumers to your content, they always bought from you? Now you can with your mapped out pricing strategy.

Customer's Perception With Your Product

The first thing you need to create a list of is the initial thought process that goes through the customer's mind when they first encounter your video.

Make two columns:

1. What are the substitutes for your video content? What are some things they might invest their time in besides your content?

2. What complements your video content well? What else will they watch along with your content?

After you make this list, then go back and make sure your content matches up to their initial thoughts. You may need to infuse emotional triggers into your videos and marketing to make it more viable for selling.

Snap Judgments Based On Your Preview

After you jot down your customer's initial thoughts, you want to go back and do some analysis around their buying behavior.

Make two columns, and list out the items:

1. What are the intuitive/gut judgments consumers will make about your content?

2. What are the rational/logical judgments they will make about your content?

When you are done creating these two lists, then go back and make sure your video content matches up to their judgment process.

People make fast decisions when it comes to online purchases. What are you going to do to grab their attention?

Perceived Value Of The Video

The next item on the to-do list is to create a value based prototype for your videos.

Your content should be heavily influenced by substitutes and complements.

For example, if your content replaces something that is $20, then you shouldn't price higher than that.

Take a moment and create a timeline around your content, look at the one on the right if you need help.

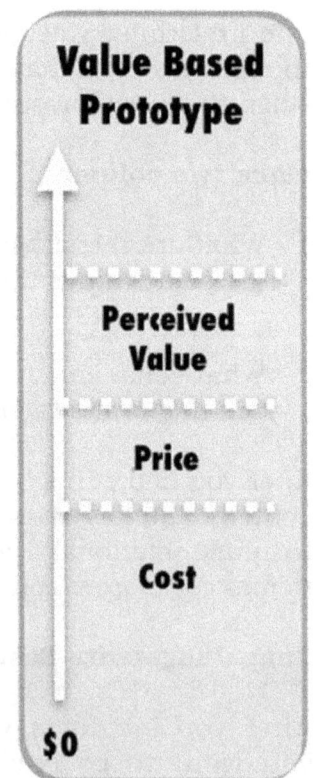

Value Based Prototype

Perceived Value

Price

Cost

$0

Your Target Segments

How broad of a market are you targeting? Create a list of three to four different cohorts or groups who will love what your video channel offers. Once you create these groups then you will be able to create videos that serve these markets specifically.

Remember:

- Customers are analytical, but they are conditioned to take leaps from logic.
- They want really great bargains and they base these on arbitrary reference points.
- They want to be as risk averse as possible with their money.
- They don't want to be on the hook if they make the wrong choices.

If you are able to manage the desires of your consumers while providing them content they are eager to pay for, you are well on your way to building an unstoppable video business.

Eventually you will have ambassadors for your brand and you will use the help of your consumer army to spread the word to others about your brand.

The content you create is far more important than the pricing. The pricing is just the barrier to your content. However, if your content isn't a fit for your audience then your video business may fail. If people love your content then you can raise your prices without question.

Focus on the value you deliver. We all know pricing is not based on the cost to produce something nor what you think the price should be. Pricing is based on the value you bring your customers, and what the customer believes the content to be worth.

CONCLUSION

Congratulations! You've made it through Video Profits: How to Create Massive Profits and a New Stream of Income With Your Video Content.

We hope that this book has given you a comprehensive way to turn your video content into a viable profit stream for you and your business.

Our goal with this book is to help as many content creators and businesses as we can turn their videos into a viable profit stream. We are passionate about giving you the best experience possible through empowering you with control over your revenue and online video management.

The future of online video selling is here, and Gbox is at the helm. We can't wait to hear about your success!

Where to next?

Start by creating your very own, customized Gbox channel[87], and get started selling your videos online.

Visit www.GboxVideoProfits.com now to gain exclusive access to even more bonus video selling resources!

We are constantly updating this resource page with the latest innovations in video selling. Marketing, email, pricing and creation strategies to help boost your videos sales.

Check out our exclusive 4-part video training series

where you will learn:

- More tools and resources for you to improve your video content.

- Bonus pricing strategies with a real life case study to see them in action.

- How this Gbox user makes over $50,000 a month selling online videos.

- How to entice thousands of viewers to view your videos.

More tools and resources for you to improve your video content.

And it's all available now for access for free! Visit:

www.GboxVideoProfits.com

HOW TO CONTACT US

For more information about VIDEO PROFITS: How to Create Massive Profits and a New Stream of Income With Your Video Content; information on speaking/ seminars/training, booking the authors to speak at your next event, or for any other reason, please contact us at our website:

www.Gbox.com

TOOLS & RESOURCES

Here is a list of all the resources and URLs cited throughout the book.

BONUS Resources For This Book:

www.GboxVideoProfits.com

Survey for your free gift: **smarturl.it/1minutesurvey**

Video Selling
• Gbox: www.gbox.com

Social Media Tools
• Hootsuite: hootsuite.com
• Buffer: bufferapp.com
• Snip.ly: snip.ly
• FollowerWonk: www.followerwonk.com
• Facebook Insights: www.facebook.com/insights
• Timely: www.timelyapp.com
• Tweetreach: tweetreach.com
• Trendsmap: trendsmap.com
• Bit.ly: bitly.com
• Intercom: www.intercom.io

Email Marketing
• Infusionsoft: www.infusionsoft.com
• GetResponse: www.getresponse.com
• AWeber: www.aweber.com

- Salesforce: http://www.salesforce.com
- Hubspot: http://www.hubspot.com
- Themeforest: themeforest.net/category/marketing/email-templates
- Campaign Monitor: www.campaignmonitor.com/email-templates/all
- Templateria: templateria.com
- Customer.io: customer.io
- GetResponse: www.getresponse.com
- MailChimp: blog.mailchimp.com/insights-from-mailchimps-send-time-optimization-system
- GitHub: github.com/seanpowell/Email-Boilerplate
- Litmus: litmus.com
- Responsive Design: litmus.com/blog/responsive-email-testing-yields-higher-click-rate-deckers
- Mail Tester: www.mail-tester.com
- Sender Score: senderscore.org
- HubSpot Email: www.hubspot.com/products/email
- Active Campaign: www.activecampaign.com
- Testing Resources: www.practicalecommerce.com/articles/4133-10-A-B-Testing-Tools-for-Small-Businesses
- Webtrends: www.webtrends.com
- Abtasty: en.abtasty.com
- Click Throo: www.clickthroo.com
- Optimizely: www.optimizely.com

Keywords & Analytics
- SEMRUSH: http://www.semrush.com

- UberSuggest: ubersuggest.org
- Learn About Google Analytics: www.analyticsacademy.withgoogle.com/explorer

Survey Tools
- Qualaroo: www.qualaroo.com
- Survey.io: www.survey.io
- SurveyMonkey: www.surveymonkey.com
- Typeform: www.typeform.com

Influencers
- Video Marketing Scholars: videomarketingscholars.gbox.com
- Andrew Chen: andrewchen.co
- Sean Ellis: Twitter.com/SeanEllis
- Neil Patel: Twitter.com/neilpatel
- Guy Kawasaki: twitter.com/GuyKawasaki
- Tim Ferris: Twitter.com/tferriss
- Fair Observer: fairobserver.gbox.com
- Gbox Featured Channels: www.gbox.com/featured
- Hull FC LIVE: www.hullfclive.tv

Other Useful Resources
- Quora: www.quora.com
- Yahoo Answers: answers.yahoo.com
- Google Hangouts: plus.google.com/hangouts
- Skype: www.skype.com/en
- LeadPages: www.leadpages.net/products

- SumoMe: wordpress.org/plugins/sumome
- Google UTM Tags: support.google.com/analytics/answer/1033867?hl=en
- Adroll: www.adroll.com
- HelloBar: www.hellobar.com

Articles

- How To Create The Perfect Viral Video Contest: www.gbox.com/build-perfect-viral-video-contest
- How To Best Launch And Market Your Viral Video Contest: http://www.gbox.com/launch-perfect-viral-video-contest
- QuickSprout: www.digitalinformationworld.com/2014/01/why-video-marketing-is-so-effective-in-2014.html
- InSivia: www.insivia.com/50-must-know-stats-about-video-animation-marketing-2013
- DigitalSherpa: www.digitalsherpa.com/blog/category/video

GLOSSARY

A/B Testing: In marketing, A/B testing is jargon for a randomized experiment with two variants, A and B, which are the control and treatment in the controlled experiment. A/B testing can be used to test for conversion rates of different landing pages, newsletter content, or advertising copy/graphics.

Alt Tag/Text: Alt text (alternative text) is generally keywords that are attributed to images to describe the image. This is used on websites and in emails to account for "broken images" or some other issue that may arise across different platforms, devices, etc.

AIDA Process: AIDA is an acronym used in marketing to describe a list of events that may occur when a prospective consumer engages with an advertisement. Attention: Attract the attention of the consumer; Interest: Interest of the consumer; Desire: convince the consumer that they want and desire the product or service to satisfy a need they have; Action: Lead customers towards taking action and/or purchasing.

Call To Action (CTA): In marketing lingo, a call to action (CTA) is usually a button or an image that provokes a response and some sort of engagement from the audience.

CAN-SPAM: There are many anti-spam laws that are in effect in countries across the world. The CAN-SPAM Act is a law in the United States that was implemented to help stop citizens from being spammed in their email.

CRM: CRM stands for "Customer Relationship Management" and refers to practices, strategies and technologies that companies can use to help organize, automate, analyze and track interactions with their customers.

Email Autoresponder: An autoresponder is a sequence of email marketing messages, sometimes referred to as a "newsletter", that gets sent to the subscribers on your email list. The order and timing they are sent out in is set up by you and functions on "auto-pilot."

Full Page Interstitial Popup: An interstitial Pop Up is an ad or a prompt that shows up before a user sees an actual webpage. The pop up ad will disappear usually when the user enters their information or clicks to "skip" or "close" the ad.

Key Performance Indicator (KPI): A key performance indicator (KPI) is a business metric used to evaluate factors that are crucial to the success of an organization. KPIs differ based on the organization and their desired outcomes. A business might be interested in net revenue or customer loyalty, whereas an educational institute would maybe want to know how many of their graduates found employment in their field of study.

Landing Page: A landing page, also sometimes called a "lead capture page" is a single web page that appears in response to clicking on a search engine result or an online advertisement.

Lead Capture: A Lead Capture is another term for the contact information you acquire from prospective customers who "opt-in" to submitting their data to you. Any potential customer whose information you capture is considered a "lead" because they may "lead" to a sale in the future.

Lead Generation: In marketing, lead generation is the generation of consumer inquiry into the products or services of a business. Leads can be created for purposes such as list building, e-newsletter acquisition or for sales leads.

Lead Magnet; "Ethical Bribe": A lead magnet is something you use to encourage potential buyers to give you their information. It is an incentive (sometimes called an "ethical bribe") that can come in many different forms (free report, discount, bonus material, etc.).

Niche Market: A niche market is the subset of the market on which a specific product or service is focused. The market niche defines the product features aimed at satisfying specific market needs, as well as the price range, production quality and the demographics that it intends to impact.

Organic Traffic: Organic traffic is traffic that comes to your website or video channel as a result of unpaid search results.

Sales Funnel: The term "sales funnel" refers to the buying process that leads customers towards purchasing your products or services. A sales funnel is divided into several steps, which differ depending on the particular sales model.

Social Media: Social media refers to websites and applications that enable users to create and share content with their friends and networks, or to participate in social networking.

Social Reach: Social reach can be defined as the total number of people you are able to reach across all various social media networks.

Target Market: The specific group of consumers at which a product or service is aimed.

Traffic: Web traffic is most simply defined as the number of visitors to your website or landing pages.

MEET THE FOUNDER

DIRK LUETH

Dirk Lueth, Film Operator
& Orchestrating Gbox.
Tweet me @dirklueth

Dirk Lueth Ph.D. is a serial entrepreneur, mentor at the German accelerator and an investor. Dirk studied Business Administration in Frankfurt and Paris.

He holds a Ph.D. from the European Business School/ Germany. He is a fluent speaker of four different languages: German, English, French and Spanish.

Dirk started his career as the co-founder of Financial Times Germany, a global brand that innovated in multiple media outlets (print and online) and won several awards. Subsequently he joined Lycos Europe where he ran the content and licenses business across 12 countries.

Thereafter he co-founded Forbatec, a financial software company, which he sold to SunGard. At SunGard he became COO of the technology group where he drove strategic acquisitions and significant business deals.

In 2012, Dirk founded OnCircle, Inc. with Stefan Roever and Michael Janssen. The company is based in the heart of Silicon Valley and develops the video monetization platform Gbox. Gbox – what this book is about - empowers creators to sell their content directly to their audience. A strong patent portfolio supports its unique and strong technology. As the founder and CEO, Dirk raised venture capital and successfully brought the platform to market.

In his active role as a mentor at the German accelerator, he has helped over 10 German companies to find US customers and get settled in the Silicon Valley. He has also supported them in their fundraising efforts. Currently, Dirk resides with his family in Menlo Park, CA and enjoys competitive swimming on International level.

MEET THE TEAM

Located in Silicon Valley, California, Gbox was created and developed by an awesome team of video enthusiasts and successful entrepreneurs. Together we applied our experience in payments and content distribution to build a video commerce platform like no other.

At the end of the day, we were brought together through our strong beliefs that the future of online content distribution is one where the creators of the best content are rewarded for their efforts.

Reach out to us on Twitter[1], Facebook[2] or by email[3].

We look forward to hearing about your video selling success!

ECKART SPEIDEL

Product specialist, driver of vision, strategy
and execution.

Tweet me @eckartspeidel

SERGEY AVERCHENKOV

VP of Engineering at Gbox, Stunt director & pyrotechnics.

Tweet me @AgentSergey

JOEL TELLO

Jedi Master with extensive experience in software development. Gbox's dev lead and sports aficionado.

Tweet me @chato_guzman

JP

Software engineer, GIF connoisseur and obsessive pixel arranger.

Tweet me @jaypeafranco

RAMSES ROSASSWAT SQA

Passionate about finding and eliminating software flaws, enthusiastic about educating others about SQA best practices.

Tweet me @ramses33ra

CARLOS ANDONAEGUI

Software addict and technology enthusiast. Gbox's backend dev padawan.

Tweet me @charlires

165

CARLOS LOPEZ

Rockstar developer. Happily located at the intersection of technology and art. Loving what I do everyday.

Tweet me @carlyeah

RAJ RAO

Aspiring polymath, information junkie, and Gbox evangelist.

Tweet me @rjkrao

SWETA PATEL

Author of three best-selling books, marketing enthusiast, Gbox's ambassador and marketing growth ninja. I love turning strangers into passionate customers.

Tweet me @SwetaSpeaks

STEVE PADDON

Focuses his energy making the Gbox product amazing. His greatest accomplishment is that his wife and children still find him funny.

Tweet me @sppaddon

PAUL MILLER

Dad, an awesome home cook, culture and technology enthusiast. I'm a huge fan of customer happiness and growth.

Tweet me @justpaulmiller

BREA WHITE

Startup enthusiast and administration specialist. Managing operations at Gbox, improving staff functionality and ramping up the team spirit.

Tweet me @brealeezy

MIKE VALERA

Designer, growth scientist and entrepreneur.

Tweet me @mikevalera

DISCLAIMER & TERMS OF USE AGREEMENT

Although the author and publisher have made every effort to ensure that the information in this book is correct at press time, the author and publisher do not assume and hereby disclaim any liability to any party for any loss, damage, or disruption caused by errors or omissions, whether such errors or omissions result from negligence, accident, or any other cause.

The author and publisher of this book disclaim all warranties (expressed or implied), merchantability or fitness for any particular purpose. The author and publisher shall in no event be held liable to any party for any direct, indirect, punitive, special, incidental or other consequential damages arising directly or indirectly from any use of this material which is provided "as is," and without warranties.

The author and publisher do not warrant the performance, effectiveness or applicability of any sites listed or linked to in this book.

All links are for informational purposes only and are not warranted for content, accuracy or any other implied or explicit purpose.

Your level of success in attaining the results claimed in our materials depends on the time you devote to implementing the strategies, ideas and techniques mentioned, your finances, knowledge and various skills. Since these factors differ according to individuals, we cannot guarantee your success or income level. Nor are we responsible for any of your actions.

BOOK ENDNOTES

[1] twitter.com/gboxapp

[2] facebook.com/GboxVideos

[3] swetapatel@gbox.com

[4] digitalinformationworld.com/2014/01/why-video-marketing-is-so-effective-in-2014.html

[5] insivia.com/50-must-know-stats-about-video-animation-marketing-2013

[6] digitalsherpa.com/blog/category/video

[7] twitter.com/tferriss

[8] twitter.com/GuyKawasaki

[9] twitter.com/NeilPatel

[10] twitter.com/SeanEllis

[11] fairobserver.gbox.com

[12] gbox.com

[13] semrush.com

[14] ubersuggest.org

[15] snip.ly

[16] qualaroo.com

[17] survey.io

[18] surveymonkey.com

[19] typeform.com

[20] ubersuggest.org

[21] plus.google.com

[22] facebook.com

[23] twitter.com

[24] followerwonk.com

[25] linkedin.com

[26] analyticsacademy.withgoogle.com/explorer

[27] buffer.com

[28] timelyapp.com

[29] hootsuite.com

[30] tweetreach.com

[31] trendsmap.com

[32] bit.ly

[33] facebook.com/insights

[34] intercom.io

[35] snip.ly

[36] quora.com

[37] answers.yahoo.com

[38] plus.google.com/hangouts

[39] skype.com

[40] infusionsoft.com

[41] getresponse.com

[42] aweber.com

[43] salesforce.com

[44] hubspot.com/products/email

[45] themeforest.net/category/marketing/email-templates

[46] campaignmonitor.com/email-templates/all

[47] templateria.com

[48] qualaroo.com

[49] andrewchen.co

[50] leadpages.net/products

[51] wordpress.org/plugins/sumome

[52] customer.io

[53] getresponse.com

[54] blog.mailchimp.com/insights-from-mailchimps-send-time-optimization-system

[55] support.google.com/analytics/answer/1033867?hl=en

[56] aweber.com

[57] mailchimp.com

[58] campaignmonitor.com

[59] hubspot.com/products/email

[60] customer.io

[61] activecampaign.com

[62] practicalecommerce.com/articles/4133-10-A-B-Testing-Tools-for-Small-Businesses

[63] gbox.com/build-perfect-viral-video-contest

[64] gbox.com/launch-perfect-viral-video-contest

[65] webtrends.com

[66] en.abtasty.com

[67] clickthroo.com

[68] optimizely.com

[69] gbox.com/featured

[70] hullfclive.tv

[71] gbox.com/build-perfect-viral-video-contest

[72] gbox.com/launch-perfect-viral-video-contest

[73] typeform.com

[74] qualaroo.com

[75] adroll.com

[76] hellobar.com

[77] themeforest.net/category/marketing/email-tcmplates

[78] github.com/seanpowell/Email-Boilerplate

[79] litmus.com

[80] litmus.com/blog/responsive-email-testing-yields-higher-click-rate-deckers

[81] mail-tester.com

[82] enderscore.org

[83] campaignmonitor.com/email-templates/all

[84] themeforest.net/category/marketing/email-templates

[85] templateria.com

[86] videomarketingscholars.gbox.com

[87] gbox.com/auth/signup

www.ingramcontent.com/pod-product-compliance
Lightning Source LLC
Chambersburg PA
CBHW051910170526

45168CB00001B/317